Christmas Gifts of Good Taste

ISBN: 0-8487-2831-9
ISSN: 1534-7788
Library of Congress Control Number: 2004105639
Printed in the United States of America
First Printing 2004

OXMOOR HOUSE, INC.
Editor in Chief: Nancy Fitzpatrick Wyatt
Executive Editor: Susan Carlisle Payne
Art Director: Cynthia Rose Cooper
Copy Chief: Allison Long Lowery

Christmas Gifts of Good Taste
Editor: Susan Ray
Assistant Editor: McCharen Pratt
Copy Editor: Diane Rose
Editorial Assistant: Dawn Russell
Senior Photographer: Jim Bathie
Photographer: Brit Huckabay
Senior Photo Stylist: Kay E. Clarke
Photo Stylist: Ashley Wyatt
Director, Test Kitchens: Elizabeth Tyler Luckett
Assistant Director, Test Kitchens: Julie Christopher
Recipe Editor: Gayle Hays Sadler
Test Kitchens Staff: Kristi Carter, Nicole Faber, Jan A. Smith,
    Elise Weis, Kelley Self Wilton
Publishing Systems Administrator: Rick Tucker
Color Specialist: Jim Sheetz
Director of Production: Phillip Lee
Production Manager: Theresa L. Beste
Production Assistant: Faye Porter Bonner

Contributors:
Copy Editor: Adrienne S. Davis
Designer and Photo Stylist: Connie Formby
Photo Stylist: Katie Stoddard
Indexer: Mary Ann Laurens

To order additional publications,
call 1-800-765-6400.
For more books to enrich your life, visit
oxmoorhouse.com

CHRISTMAS GIFTS of GOOD TASTE

This Christmas, delight friends and family with delicious gifts from the kitchen that are cleverly packaged. With over 130 recipes, there's something for everyone on your list. Sweet treats like the *Orange-Nut Balls* featured on page 46 and the *Rum Fudge Cakes* on page 84 will get rave reviews. The snackers on your list will go nuts over the *Curried Party Mix* on page 90 and the *Grab 'n' Go Gorp* on page 106. And no one can resist the *Triple Chocolate Cake* on page 154.

In addition to a quick—and great-looking—packaging idea that comes with each recipe, you'll find even more gift-wrapping tips sprinkled throughout these pages. We hope this volume chock-full of handmade pleasures helps you create your most memorable Christmas ever.

The Editors

Oxmoor House®

TABLE OF CONTENTS

TOILE LA LA LA LA

Cinnamon-flavored chips make these cookies a delicious departure from ordinary chocolate chip cookies. Get a head start on your holiday gifts by making this slice-and-bake cookie dough in October, and then freezing it. To give, wrap the logs in decorative wax paper, and tie the ends with ribbon. Don't forget to include baking instructions!

CINNAMON CHIP ICEBOX COOKIES

1	cup butter or margarine, softened
2	cups sugar
2	large eggs
2	teaspoons vanilla extract
4	cups all-purpose flour
1	(10-ounce) package cinnamon chips (we tested with Hershey's)
1	cup chopped pecans, toasted

Beat butter at medium speed with an electric mixer until creamy. Gradually add sugar, beating well. Add eggs and vanilla, beating until blended. Gradually add flour, beating at low speed just until blended. Stir in cinnamon chips and pecans.

Divide dough into 3 portions; roll each portion into a 12-inch log. Wrap each log in wax paper. Chill 8 hours or up to 3 days, or freeze in an airtight container up to 3 months. *Yield:* 3 gift logs (4 dozen cookies each).

Directions for recipe card: To bake cookies, preheat oven to 350 degrees. Cut log into 48 (¼-inch-thick) slices, and place slices on ungreased baking sheets.

Bake for 10 to 12 minutes or until edges are lightly browned. Cool on baking sheets 5 minutes. Remove to wire racks to cool completely. *Yield:* 4 dozen.

Note: Cookie dough may also be dropped by rounded tablespoonfuls, 2 inches apart, onto ungreased baking sheets, and then baked.

Computer Creations
Make all kinds of recipe cards and gift tags on your computer. Experiment with different fonts and clip art images to design your own cards. You'll save time by making multiple tags, and recipients will love the creative touch.

HOW SWEET IT IS

This easy-to-make sweet-hot mustard tastes great with pretzels, egg rolls, or on sandwiches. Pour it into a cute jar, tie with a ribbon, and attach a handmade gift tag for a colorful presentation. Deliver it along with gourmet pretzels for immediate indulgence.

SWEET TANGY MUSTARD

1 (14-ounce) can sweetened condensed milk
1 (8-ounce) bottle prepared mustard
2 tablespoons prepared horseradish
2 tablespoons Worcestershire sauce

Stir together all ingredients in a medium bowl. Store in glass container in refrigerator up to 3 months.
Yield: 2⅓ cups.

CANS OF COOKIES

Crushed fennel seeds give these buttery cookies a faint licorice flavor. The sturdy little cookies travel well in recycled potato chip cans.

FENNEL COOKIES

1	cup unsalted butter, softened
1	cup sugar
2	large eggs
3	cups all-purpose flour
1	teaspoon baking powder
½	teaspoon salt
2	tablespoons fennel seeds, crushed
1	tablespoon vanilla extract

Sugar or turbinado sugar

Beat butter at medium speed with an electric mixer until creamy; gradually add 1 cup sugar, beating until light and fluffy. Add eggs, 1 at a time, beating until blended after each addition.

Combine flour, baking powder, and salt; add to butter mixture, beating just until blended. Stir in fennel seeds and vanilla.

Divide dough into 2 portions; roll each portion into a 12-inch log on wax paper. Freeze 2 hours or until firm.

Preheat oven to 350 degrees.

Cut each log into ¼-inch-thick slices, using a sharp knife; place slices on ungreased baking sheets. Sprinkle cookies with desired sugar. Bake for 10 to 11 minutes or until edges are barely golden. Cool 1 minute on baking sheets; remove to wire racks to cool.

Yield: 8 dozen.

Canned Goods

Recycle potato chip cans for clever Christmas packages. Cut a piece of wrapping paper large enough to wrap the entire can. Glue the paper to the outside of the can.

VISIONS OF BLUEBERRIES

*I*magine plump blueberries
and just the right amount of tangy
lemon juice and rind to create this
fresh sauce. It's the perfect partner
for fluffy buttermilk pancakes or
scoops of creamy vanilla ice cream.
Package it in a syrup container
trimmed with holiday stickers.

BLUEBERRY SAUCE

3   cups fresh blueberries
1   cup cold water
⅔   cup sugar
2   tablespoons cornstarch
¼   teaspoon grated lemon
      rind
1½   tablespoons fresh lemon
      juice

Combine first 4 ingredients in a
medium saucepan; bring to a boil
over medium heat, and boil 1
minute, stirring constantly.

Remove from heat, and stir in
lemon rind and lemon juice. Store
in refrigerator. Serve sauce warm
over pancakes or waffles, or serve
chilled over ice cream, angel food
cake, or cheesecake.
Yield: 3 cups.

DRAW STRAWS

This cheese straw recipe can be shaped with a cookie press or rolled into a log and sliced into disks. Deliver the treats in boxes tied with ribbon.

EASY-AS-PIE CHEESE STRAWS

1   (11-ounce) package piecrust mix (we tested with Betty Crocker)
1   (5-ounce) jar sharp process cheese spread
¼   teaspoon ground red pepper

Process piecrust mix and remaining ingredients in a food processor 30 seconds or until mixture forms a ball, stopping to scrape down sides.

Divide dough in half, and form each portion into a 7-inch log; wrap in plastic wrap, and chill 1 hour.

Preheat oven to 375 degrees.

Cut dough into ¼-inch slices. Press dough with a fork to create a crisscross pattern. Place cheese straws on lightly greased baking sheets.

Bake for 8 to 10 minutes or until lightly browned. Transfer to wire racks to cool.
Yield: 5 dozen.

Cheese Straw Success
- For flaky cheese straws, don't overmix the dough.
- Portion dough ahead, and keep the remainder chilled until ready to use. If dough gets soft, refrigerate 10 to 15 minutes.
- Shiny baking sheets yield a golden-brown color. Food placed on dark baking sheets cooks faster and sometimes overbrowns.
- Set your timer for 1 to 2 minutes less than the recommended baking time, as oven temperatures tend to vary.
- Place cheese straws between sheets of wax paper, and store them in tightly sealed tins and containers.

TASTE OF THE TROPICS

The combination of golden raisins, dried pineapple, coconut, and honey will elicit fantasies of palm trees and hula skirts. Transport a friend to the tropical isles with a gift of this granola. You can make it and freeze it three months in advance. Fill clamp-top jars with handfuls of mix and tie with a colorful ribbon and gift tag.

TROPICAL GRANOLA

⅓	cup honey
¼	cup canola oil
5	cups uncooked regular oats
1	cup flaked coconut
½	cup macadamia nuts, chopped
½	cup sunflower kernels
½	cup honey crunch wheat germ
¼	cup sesame seeds
½	cup chopped dried pineapple
½	cup golden raisins

Preheat oven to 300 degrees.

Stir together honey and oil in a large bowl. Stir in oats and next 5 ingredients. Spoon mixture onto 2 ungreased 15- x 10-inch jellyroll pans.

Bake for 30 minutes or until golden, stirring every 10 minutes. Cool completely in pans on wire racks. Pour into a large bowl. Stir in pineapple and raisins. Store in an airtight container up to 2 weeks, or freeze up to 3 months. *Yield:* 8 cups.

Merry Christmas
From Our House
to Yours

SHORTBREAD BONUS

Everybody's favorite sandwich cookie appears where you'd least expect it—crushed and stirred into another cookie. Surprise friends with a stack of this shortbread.

COOKIES 'N' CREAM SHORTBREAD

1   cup butter, softened
½   cup sugar
¼   teaspoon vanilla extract
2¼   cups all-purpose flour
⅛   teaspoon salt
14   chocolate sandwich
       cookies, coarsely
       crumbled (1½ cups)
       (we tested with Oreos)

Preheat oven to 275 degrees. Beat butter at medium speed with an electric mixer until creamy; gradually add sugar, beating well. Stir in vanilla.

Combine flour and salt; gradually add to butter mixture, beating at low speed until blended.

Stack 'Em Up
For an unexpected presentation, consider cutting cookies in graduated sizes by using different-size cookie cutters or round glasses. Check out flea markets—or even department stores—for brightly colored, vintage plates to stack the cookies on, and match ribbons to the plates.

Fold in cookie crumbs. (The more you blend the cookie crumbs into the dough, the darker it gets. If you want a lightly marbled shortbread, barely stir in crumbs.)

Roll dough to ½-inch thickness on a lightly floured surface. Cut with a 2½-inch round or Christmas cutter (or see box below for cutting graduated sizes). Place 2 inches apart on ungreased baking sheets.

Bake for 45 to 48 minutes or until bottoms barely begin to brown. Cool 1 minute on baking sheets. Remove to wire racks to cool. *Yield:* about 1½ dozen.

CHOCOLATE INDULGENCE

A chocolate, chesslike filling snuggles peanuts in this scrumptious tart. A purchased golden plate highlights this chocolate treat—and will be a great holiday serving piece once the dessert is gone.

BOURBON-CHOCOLATE-PECAN TART

½ (15-ounce) package refrigerated piecrusts
1¼ cups sugar
½ cup water
⅔ cup heavy whipping cream, warmed
3 tablespoons bourbon
¼ cup butter or margarine, melted
1 large egg, lightly beaten
1¼ cups pecans, toasted
¾ cup semisweet chocolate morsels
1 cup semisweet chocolate morsels for drizzle (optional)

Fit piecrust into a greased 9-inch tart pan with a removable bottom.

Combine sugar and water in a medium saucepan; bring to a boil, stirring constantly until sugar dissolves. Reduce heat to medium-high, and boil, without stirring, 7 to 8 minutes or until syrup is golden, swirling pan occasionally. (Wash down sides of pan with water, using a pastry brush, if sugar crystals form on sides.)

Remove from heat, and gradually stir in warm cream and bourbon (mixture will bubble up). Cool completely (about 35 minutes).

Preheat oven to 375 degrees.

Add butter and egg, stirring until smooth. Stir in pecans and chocolate morsels. Pour mixture into prepared crust.

Bake for 36 to 38 minutes. Cool completely in pan on a wire rack.

To make chocolate drizzle, place chocolate morsels in a small zip-top freezer bag; seal. Submerge in hot water until chocolate melts, kneading gently to blend. Snip a tiny hole in 1 corner of bag, and drizzle over tart.

Yield: 1 (9-inch) tart.

ORANGE DELIGHTS

Prepare and freeze this breakfast favorite up to a month in advance. Deliver the scones on a painted Christmas plate. It's simple to make—just use enamel or ceramic paint to create swirls and dots around the rim of the plate, and let dry.

ORANGE-PECAN SCONES

- 2 cups self-rising flour
- ½ cup sugar
- 2 teaspoons grated orange rind
- ⅓ cup butter or margarine
- ½ cup buttermilk
- ¼ cup fresh orange juice
- ½ cup chopped pecans
- 1 teaspoon vanilla extract

Sugar

Preheat oven to 425 degrees.

Combine first 3 ingredients. Cut butter into flour mixture with a pastry blender until crumbly; add buttermilk and next 3 ingredients, stirring just until dry ingredients are moistened.

Turn dough out onto a lightly floured surface, and knead 3 or 4 times.

Pat dough into a 7-inch circle, and place on a lightly greased baking sheet. Cut into 8 wedges; sprinkle evenly with sugar.

Bake for 14 to 16 minutes or until golden brown. Serve warm or let cool and freeze up to 1 month. *Yield:* 8 scones.

Directions for recipe card: Store at room temperature up to 2 days, or freeze up to 1 month. Reheat scones at 350 degrees for 10 minutes or until thoroughly heated.

Push peanut butter cups into the centers of these scrumptious cookies while they're still hot. Then stack the cooled cookies inside a napkin-lined wire basket, and trim with a ribbon. For a festive touch, bake the cookies in seasonal muffin liners, which can be found in most kitchen shops.

PEANUT BUTTER CUP COOKIES

½	cup sugar
⅓	cup creamy peanut butter
¼	cup butter or margarine, softened
1	large egg
2	tablespoons whipping cream
1	teaspoon vanilla extract
1	cup all-purpose flour
1	teaspoon baking soda
⅛	teaspoon salt
½	cup chopped unsalted peanuts
1	(13-ounce) package miniature peanut butter cup candies (we tested with Reese's)

Preheat oven to 350 degrees. Beat first 3 ingredients at medium speed with an electric mixer 2 minutes. Add egg, whipping cream, and vanilla; beat well. Combine flour, soda, and salt. Add to peanut butter mixture; stir well. Stir in peanuts.

Roll dough into 1-inch balls. Press dough into miniature (1¾-inch) muffin pans lined with paper muffin cups. Bake for 12 minutes. Remove from oven; press down centers with thumb and press a peanut butter cup into center of each cookie. Bake for 3 more minutes. Remove from oven. Cool completely in pan on a wire rack.
Yield: 3 dozen.

PECANS APLENTY

Pecan halves get a toasting and a bit of spice, courtesy of cinnamon, red pepper, and hot sauce. Package the nibbles in an airtight container, and give them to your neighbor as a holiday remembrance.

HOT 'N' SPICY PECANS

3	tablespoons butter or margarine, melted
3	tablespoons white wine Worcestershire sauce
1	teaspoon seasoned salt
½	teaspoon ground red pepper
½	teaspoon ground cinnamon

Dash of hot sauce
4	cups pecan halves

Preheat oven to 300 degrees.

Stir together first 6 ingredients in a large bowl. Add pecans, and toss gently to coat. Place in an ungreased 15- x 10-inch jelly-roll pan.

Bake for 20 to 25 minutes, stirring twice. Cool completely. Store in an airtight container. *Yield:* 4 cups.

Cloaked in Cloth

Cloth covers are easy to create. Place the container on top of a piece of fabric (we used mesh) that's trimmed so that it wraps to the top of the container. Tie with cording or ribbon.

THIS ONE TAKES THE CAKE

*B*ake this decadent cake in a disposable pan, wrap with ribbon, and deliver to a friend along with a jar of caramel sauce for extra indulgence. Gift wrapping doesn't get any easier.

CHOCOLATE-CARAMEL-NUT SURPRISE CAKE

1   (18.25-ounce) package German chocolate cake mix with pudding (we tested with Pillsbury)
1   (14-ounce) package caramels
½   cup butter or margarine
⅓   cup milk
1   cup chopped dry-roasted peanuts
¾   cup milk chocolate morsels
Caramel sauce (optional)

Preheat oven to 350 degrees.

Prepare cake mix according to package directions. Pour half of batter into a greased and floured 13- x 9-inch pan. Bake for 10 minutes. (Cake will not test done.) Cool cake on a wire rack 10 minutes.

Meanwhile, unwrap caramels. Combine caramels, butter, and milk in a heavy saucepan, and cook over medium heat until caramels melt, stirring often. Spread over cake.

Sprinkle peanuts and chocolate morsels over caramel mixture. Spread remaining cake batter evenly over top. Bake for 25 to 30 more minutes. Cool in pan on wire rack. Cut into squares. Drizzle with caramel sauce, if desired. *Yield:* 15 servings.

NUTS FOR ORANGE

This recipe makes a sturdy little cookie and yields extras for you to keep and serve with hot orange tea. Purchase bakery boxes with cellophane windows to reveal a glimpse of these pretty cookies. Tie the handles with raffia or ribbon and add a gift tag.

ORANGE-DATE-NUT COOKIES

1 (10-ounce) package dried chopped dates
1 teaspoon grated orange rind
1 tablespoon orange juice
1 cup butter or margarine, softened
1½ cups sugar
1 large egg
1 teaspoon vanilla extract
2½ cups all-purpose flour
1½ teaspoons baking powder
½ teaspoon salt
1 cup finely chopped toasted pecans, divided

Line a 9- x 5-inch loafpan with aluminum foil, allowing foil to extend over edges of pan, and set aside.

Position knife blade in food processor bowl; add first 3 ingredients. Process 45 seconds or until dates are finely chopped. Set aside.

Beat butter at medium speed with a heavy-duty electric mixer until blended. Gradually add sugar, beating until blended. Add egg and vanilla; beat well. Combine flour, baking powder, and salt; gradually add to butter mixture, beating at low speed just until blended.

Divide dough into 3 portions. Knead ½ cup pecans into 1 portion of dough; press into prepared pan. Knead date mixture into 1 portion of dough; press into pan over pecan mixture. Knead remaining ½ cup pecans into remaining portion of dough; press into pan over date mixture. Cover and chill at least 2 hours.

Preheat oven to 350 degrees.

Invert loafpan onto a cutting board, removing and discarding aluminum foil. Cut dough lengthwise into 3 sections. Cut

each section of dough crosswise into ¼-inch slices. Place slices 1½ inches apart on lightly greased baking sheets.

Bake for 14 to 15 minutes or until lightly browned. Cool slightly. Remove to wire racks to cool completely.
Yield: 8 dozen.

SEEING RED

Dried tomatoes give this pesto its ruby hue and intense tomato flavor. Accompany a jar of the robust spread with a fresh baguette or toasted baguette slices.

RED PESTO

1⅔ cups (3 ounces) dried
        tomatoes
¼   cup grated Parmesan cheese
1   cup loosely packed fresh
        Italian parsley
4   garlic cloves
¾   cup extra-virgin olive oil
Toasted French baguette slices

Place dried tomatoes in a small bowl; add boiling water to cover, and let stand 5 minutes. Drain and pat dry. Place tomatoes, cheese, parsley, and garlic in food processor bowl. With processor running, slowly pour oil through food chute, processing until smooth. Chill in airtight containers up to 1 week. Serve with toasted French baguette slices.
Yield: 1⅔ cups.

Fringed Bread Tin
For the bread container, lightly paint an elongated tin container, and let it dry. Then hot-glue eyelash fringe around the top of the tin, and stuff with tissue.

CANDY COOKIES

White chocolate, nuts, and chocolate-covered caramel candies pack these cookies with dynamite flavor. Stack them inside colorful gift sacks tied with ribbon, and add a gift tag.

WHITE CHOCOLATE, PEANUT, AND CARAMEL CANDY COOKIES

1	cup butter or margarine, softened
1	cup granulated sugar
1	cup firmly packed light brown sugar
2	large eggs
1	teaspoon vanilla extract
2½	cups uncooked regular oats
2	cups all-purpose flour
1	teaspoon baking powder
½	teaspoon baking soda
½	teaspoon salt
3	(1.91-ounce) packages chocolate-coated caramels, chilled and chopped (we tested with Rolo)
2	(4-ounce) white chocolate bars, chopped (we tested with Ghirardelli)
1½	cups unsalted peanuts, chopped

Preheat oven to 375 degrees.

Beat butter at medium speed with an electric mixer until creamy; add sugars, beating well. Add eggs and vanilla, beating until blended.

Process oats in a blender or food processor until finely ground. Combine oats, flour, and next 3 ingredients; add to butter mixture, beating well. Stir in chopped candy, white chocolate, and peanuts.

Shape dough into 1½-inch balls, and place on parchment paper-lined baking sheets.

Bake for 10 minutes or until lightly browned. Cool 1 minute on baking sheets. Remove to wire racks to cool completely.
Yield: 6 dozen.

Note: Find chocolate-coated caramels at your local drug store on the candy aisle. The candies may make the cookies stick slightly to the baking sheet. That's why we recommend baking these on parchment paper.

WRAP 'N' ROLL

Chili-coated cheese logs make a flavor-packed gift. This recipe makes two logs, so you can keep one for yourself and pass one along to a friend.

GARLIC-CHEESE LOGS

2	(3-ounce) packages cream cheese, softened
1	tablespoon mayonnaise
1	tablespoon Worcestershire sauce
1	or 2 garlic cloves, crushed
1	teaspoon dry mustard
¼	teaspoon salt
¼	teaspoon hot sauce
4	cups (16 ounces) shredded sharp Cheddar cheese
1	tablespoon paprika
1½	teaspoons chili powder

Combine first 7 ingredients in a large mixing bowl; beat at medium speed with an electric mixer until creamy. Gradually add Cheddar cheese, mixing until blended.

Divide mixture in half, and shape each portion into an 8-inch log. Combine paprika and chili powder; roll logs in spice mixture.

Cover and chill 8 hours or until ready to serve. Thinly slice, and serve with crackers.
Yield: 2 (8-inch) logs.

Roll With It
Use a holiday stamp and ink pad to create a festive design on a sheet of parchment paper. Wrap the cheese logs in the decorated parchment paper, and tie the ends with ribbon.

CAN-DO COCOA

*H*ere's a hot cocoa mix guaranteed to contribute to daily calcium requirements. Many prepackaged mixes don't offer that advantage. This recipe makes a large yield, so you'll have lots of gifts for loved ones. Include the serving instructions with the gift.

HOT COCOA MIX

3   (9.6-ounce) packages instant nonfat dry milk powder (11½ cups)
1   (16-ounce) package powdered sugar, sifted
2   (8-ounce) cans unsweetened cocoa
1   (6-ounce) jar powdered nondairy coffee creamer
Marshmallows (optional)

Combine first 4 ingredients; stir well. Store in an airtight container. *Yield:* 15 cups mix.

Directions for recipe card: Place ¼ cup cocoa mix in a mug; add boiling water, and stir to dissolve. Top with marshmallows, if desired.

Can-Do Wrap
Keep and refill recyclable cans and jars that ingredients came in to make handy gift containers. Glue strips of ribbon around the top and bottom of the container. To label the container, cut a strip of cardstock, write the recipe name on the paper, and glue it around the center of the container.

BURST OF ORANGE

Orange curd is a luscious, superthick dessert sauce infused with the essence of citrus. Package it in a jar tied with ribbon, along with suggestions for serving over pound cake or for making the recipe for Orange Tarts, which is listed below.

ORANGE CURD

5	large eggs
3	egg yolks
½	cup sugar
5	tablespoons frozen orange juice concentrate, thawed and undiluted
2	tablespoons grated orange zest
⅛	teaspoon salt
1	cup unsalted butter, cut into small pieces
2	tablespoons Triple Sec or orange juice
2	tablespoons orange extract

Combine first 6 ingredients in top of a double boiler; bring water to a boil. Reduce heat to low, and cook, stirring constantly with a whisk, until thickened. Add butter, 1 piece at a time, stirring constantly. Stir in liqueur and extract. Spoon into a glass container; cool completely.

Store curd in a tightly covered glass container in refrigerator up to 2 weeks. Serve over pound cake, or use as a filling for a layer cake. *Yield:* 3 cups.

Orange Tarts

1	recipe Sweet Flaky Pastry
3	(1-ounce) semisweet chocolate baking squares, melted
1	cup Orange Curd

Preheat oven to 400 degrees. Roll each portion of pastry to ⅛-inch thickness on a lightly floured surface; cut into 12 equal portions. Fit into 2-inch tartlet tins; trim excess from edges, and prick bottoms with a fork. Place tins on a baking sheet.

Bake for 15 to 17 minutes or until lightly browned. Cool in tins. Carefully remove from tins, and brush chocolate inside shells; spoon 1 teaspoon curd into each shell. *Yield:* 4 dozen.

Sweet Flaky Pastry

3	cups all-purpose flour
½	cup sugar
1	cup butter
½	cup ice water

Combine flour and sugar in a large bowl; cut in butter with a pastry blender until mixture is crumbly.

Sprinkle ice water, 1 tablespoon at a time, evenly over surface; stir with a fork just until dry ingredients are moistened.

Divide dough into 4 equal portions; wrap each portion of dough in plastic wrap, and chill 8 hours. *Yield:* enough for 4 dozen tarts.

NUTS FOR CHRISTMAS

Stir up this huge batch of snack mix, package it in clear canisters, and pass it out to all your friends and neighbors. This recipe is great because it uses the entire packages of cereals and crackers it's made with.

NUTTY SNACK MIX

1	(16-ounce) package crisp wheat cereal squares (we tested with Wheat Chex)
1	(13-ounce) package baked snack crackers (we tested with Cheese Nips)
1	(12-ounce) package corn-and-rice cereal (we tested with Crispix)
1	(10-ounce) package toasted oat O-shaped cereal (we tested with Cheerios)
6	cups small pretzel twists
1	pound pecan halves
1	(16-ounce) can cocktail peanuts
2½	cups butter or margarine, melted
¼	cup Worcestershire sauce
2	tablespoons garlic powder
1½	tablespoons onion salt
1½	tablespoons celery salt
½	teaspoon ground red pepper

Preheat oven to 225 degrees. Combine first 7 ingredients in a large roasting pan. Stir together butter and remaining 5 ingredients; pour over cereal mixture, and toss well.

Cover mixture and bake for 1 hour. Uncover mixture and bake 1 more hour, stirring mixture occasionally. Cool completely. Store snack mix in airtight containers. *Yield:* 42 cups.

Note: We baked the snack mix in a 16- x 12-inch roasting pan and the pan was full. You can use 2 smaller roasting pans, but keep in mind the baking time will be less.

MERRY MUFFINS

*P*ackage these moist, tender muffins in reusable cloth sacks. Recipients can enjoy them as a sweet start to the day or as an afternoon snack. These freeze well, so they're a great make-ahead gift.

PECAN PIE MUFFINS

1   cup chopped pecans
1   cup firmly packed brown
    sugar
½   cup all-purpose flour
2   large eggs
½   cup butter or margarine,
    melted

Preheat oven to 350 degrees.

Combine first 3 ingredients in a large bowl; make a well in center.

Beat eggs until foamy. Stir in butter; add to dry ingredients, stirring just until moistened.

Place paper muffin cups in muffin pans, and coat paper cups with cooking spray; spoon batter into cups, filling three-fourths full.

Bake for 17 to 18 minutes or until done. Remove from pans immediately, and cool on wire racks.

Yield: 8 muffins.

TIN SEALED

Dense and fudgy brownies are splashed with bourbon while hot from the oven and allowed to cool to let the flavor soak in. Then they're frosted twice—once with a creamy almond frosting, then again with melted chocolate morsels.

BOURBON BROWNIES

- 2 large eggs
- ⅓ cup vegetable oil
- ¼ cup water
- 1 (21-ounce) package family-style brownie mix (we tested with Duncan Hines)
- 1 cup chopped pecans
- ⅓ cup bourbon
- ½ cup butter or margarine, softened
- 2¼ cups sifted powdered sugar
- 1 teaspoon almond extract
- 1 cup semisweet chocolate morsels
- 1 tablespoon shortening

Preheat oven to 350 degrees.

Line a 13- x 9-inch pan with aluminum foil; lightly grease foil, and set aside.

Beat eggs, oil, and water at medium speed with an electric mixer 1 minute. Gradually add brownie mix, beating well. Stir in pecans. Pour batter into prepared pan. Bake for 28 minutes. Sprinkle bourbon evenly over hot brownie layer. Chill 1 hour. Remove brownie layer from pan. Remove foil, and place brownie layer on an ungreased baking sheet.

Beat butter at medium speed until creamy; add powdered sugar and almond extract, beating until smooth. Spread frosting over brownie layer. Chill 1 hour.

Combine chocolate morsels and shortening in a microwave-safe bowl; microwave at HIGH 1½ to 2 minutes or until melted, stirring until smooth.

Cool 5 minutes, and spread over frosting layer. Chill 30 minutes. Cut into bars.

Yield: 2 dozen.

Designer Tins
Add some pizzazz to plain tins by gluing on colorful construction paper and a large label. Line the tins with cellophane.

CHEERY AND BRIGHT

Chocolate-covered cherries have some competition. This easy fudge recipe contains a sweet cherry in every square.

MERRY CHERRY FUDGE

36	maraschino cherries with stems
1	(12-ounce) package semisweet chocolate morsels
6	(1-ounce) bittersweet chocolate baking squares, chopped
1	(14-ounce) can sweetened condensed milk
1	teaspoon maraschino cherry juice
1	cup chopped pecans

Lightly coat an 8-inch square pan with cooking spray. Set aside. Blot cherries dry with paper towels.

Combine chocolates in a heavy saucepan; place over very low heat, and stir constantly until melted and smooth. Remove from heat, and stir in sweetened condensed milk and cherry juice. Stir in pecans. Spoon mixture into prepared pan. Immediately press cherries into fudge, leaving top of each cherry exposed. Cover and chill fudge 2 hours or until firm.

Cut fudge into 36 squares. Store in airtight container in refrigerator. *Yield:* 2 pounds.

Lots of Dots
Paint an assortment of festive papier-mâché boxes to fill with gifts like fudge and cookies. You can paint them in solid colors, and then add stripes or polka dots. Cut a sheet of tissue paper with decorative-edge craft scissors to line the boxes, and wrap them with ribbon to keep them closed.

FESTIVE FOCACCIA

Deliver this popular Italian flatbread on a cutting board for a gift that lasts after the holidays. A great "ripping" bread meant to be torn into serving-size pieces, it can be enjoyed alone or made into gourmet sandwiches.

ROSEMARY FOCACCIA

2	(¼-ounce) envelopes active dry yeast
2	cups warm water (100 to 110 degrees)
6	cups all-purpose flour, divided
½	cup unsalted butter, softened
½	cup finely chopped fresh rosemary, divided
1	teaspoon salt
¼	cup olive oil, divided
8	garlic cloves, minced
1	tablespoon diced pimiento
2½	teaspoons kosher salt
½	teaspoon freshly ground pepper

Combine yeast and warm water in a 4-cup glass measuring cup; let stand 5 minutes.

Place 5 cups flour in a large bowl; make a well in center. Add yeast mixture; stir until a soft dough forms.

Cover and let rise in a warm place (85 degrees), free from drafts, 45 minutes or until doubled in bulk. (Dough will be spongy.)

Sprinkle remaining 1 cup flour on a flat surface. Turn dough out onto floured surface; knead until flour is incorporated to make a firm dough. Gradually knead in butter, ¼ cup rosemary, and 1 teaspoon salt.

Knead until dough is smooth and elastic (about 9 minutes), adding additional flour, if necessary.

Brush 2 (15- x 10-inch) jellyroll pans with 1 tablespoon oil each. Divide dough in half. Press each portion into a jellyroll pan. Cover and let rise in a warm place, free from drafts, 30 to 45 minutes or until dough is almost doubled in bulk.

Preheat oven to 375 degrees.

Using fingertips, dimple the dough all over in both pans; sprinkle with minced garlic, diced pimiento, and remaining ¼ cup rosemary. Drizzle with remaining 2 tablespoons olive oil, and sprinkle with kosher salt and pepper.

Bake for 25 to 30 minutes or until golden. Cut or tear into squares.

Yield: 2 flatbreads (8 servings each).

KICKY LITTLE COOKIES

Ground ginger and pepper (yes, pepper) spice up this sugar-coated cookie that kids and adults alike will devour.

SPICY CHOCOLATE CRACKLES

1	(18.25-ounce) package devil's food cake mix
⅓	cup vegetable oil
2	large eggs, lightly beaten
1	tablespoon ground ginger
½	teaspoon pepper
1	tablespoon water
¾	cup semisweet chocolate mini-morsels
¼	cup sugar

Preheat oven to 375 degrees.

Combine first 6 ingredients in a large bowl, stirring until smooth. Stir in mini-morsels.

Shape dough into 1-inch balls; roll in sugar to coat. Place balls 2 inches apart on lightly greased baking sheets.

Bake for 9 minutes. Cool 2 to 3 minutes on baking sheets. Remove to wire racks to cool completely. *Yield:* 4 dozen.

Pack in a Stack
Wrap stacks of sturdy cookies in cellophane bags, and tie with colorful ribbon. Present stacks individually, or place a few in a small basket.

IN THE BAG

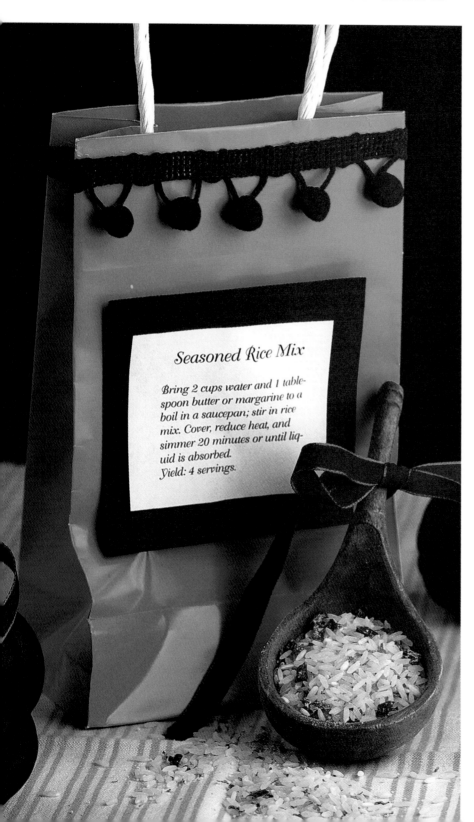

This savory rice mix makes enough for three gifts. Seal the mix in zip-top freezer bags, and place them in gift sacks decorated with pom-pom fringe. Add recipe cards that include directions for cooking the tasty blend.

SEASONED RICE MIX

3	cups uncooked long-grain rice
¼	cup dried parsley flakes
2	tablespoons chicken bouillon granules
2	tablespoons red bell pepper flakes
2	teaspoons onion powder
½	teaspoon garlic powder
¼	teaspoon dried thyme

Stir together all ingredients. Place 1 cup mixture into each of 3 airtight containers. Store in a cool, dry place.
Yield: 3 gift packages (1 cup mix each).

Directions for recipe card: Bring 2 cups water and 1 tablespoon butter or margarine to a boil in a saucepan; stir in rice mix. Cover, reduce heat, and simmer 20 minutes or until liquid is absorbed.
Yield: 4 servings.

SPREAD WITH CHEER

Green chiles and pimientos add Christmas color—and a zip of flavor—to this cheesy spread that's great on crackers or sandwiches.

GREEN CHILE-PIMIENTO CHEESE

2   (8-ounce) blocks extra sharp Cheddar cheese, shredded
1   (8-ounce) block Monterey Jack cheese with peppers, shredded
1   cup mayonnaise
1   (4.5-ounce) can chopped green chiles
1   (4-ounce) jar diced pimiento, drained
1   poblano chile pepper, seeded and minced
¼   small sweet onion, minced
2   teaspoons Worcestershire sauce

Stir together all ingredients. Cover and chill up to a week. *Yield:* about 6 cups.

Quick Jar Dress-Up
Cut four squares out of cardstock paper and write the recipe name on them, or decorate them with a Christmas design. Glue the paper labels onto square-shaped jars, and tie with a ribbon and gift tag.

SWEET SWIRLS

Just about anyone on your gift list will appreciate a loaf of homemade bread swirled with cinnamon and raisins and drizzled with a sugar glaze. Wrap the bread loosely with cellophane and ribbon, and include an ornament for a special touch.

CINNAMON LOAVES

1	(¼-ounce) envelope active dry yeast
1	cup warm water (100 to 110 degrees)
3	tablespoons granulated sugar
2	tablespoons shortening
1	large egg
½	teaspoon salt
3	to 3½ cups all-purpose flour
¼	cup butter or margarine, melted
2	tablespoons granulated sugar
2	teaspoons ground cinnamon
⅔	cup raisins
2	cups sifted powdered sugar
2	to 3 tablespoons milk
½	cup chopped pecans

Combine yeast and warm water in a 1-cup glass measuring cup; let stand 5 minutes. Combine yeast mixture, 3 tablespoons sugar, shortening, egg, salt, and half of flour in a large bowl; beat at low speed with an electric mixer until smooth. Gradually stir in enough remaining flour to make a soft dough.

Place dough in a well-greased bowl, turning to grease top. Cover and let rise in a warm place (85 degrees), free from drafts, 1 hour or until doubled in bulk, or cover and store in refrigerator up to 4 days. (If chilled, let dough return to room temperature before proceeding.)

Punch dough down; turn out onto a lightly floured surface, and knead 8 to 10 times.

Divide dough in half, keeping 1 portion covered. Roll 1 portion dough into a 15- x 7-inch rectangle on a lightly floured surface; brush with half of melted butter to within ½ inch of edges. Combine 2 tablespoons sugar and cinnamon; sprinkle half of mixture over butter. Sprinkle ⅓ cup raisins over top. Roll up, jellyroll fashion, starting at narrow edge. Pinch seams and ends together. Place loaf, seam side down, in a greased 8½- x 4½-inch loafpan. Repeat with remaining ingredients.

Cover and let rise in a warm place, free from drafts, 40 minutes or until doubled in bulk.

Preheat oven to 350 degrees.

Bake for 30 to 35 minutes or until loaves sound hollow when tapped. Remove from pans, and cool on a wire rack.

Combine powdered sugar and milk, stirring until smooth. Drizzle evenly over loaves, and sprinkle with pecans.
Yield: 2 loaves.

NUTS SO SPICY

Save the containers that these nuts come in to make great gift packages—just glue some ribbon around the cans and write messages on the lids.

JALAPEÑO NUT MIX

2   (11.5-ounce) containers unsalted mixed nuts
¼   cup butter or margarine
⅓   cup jalapeño pepper sauce
1   tablespoon hot sauce
1   tablespoon Worcestershire sauce
1½   teaspoons garlic powder
1½   teaspoons salt
1   teaspoon dry mustard

Preheat oven to 325 degrees.
Place nuts in an ungreased
15- x 10-inch jellyroll pan; reserve
cans and lids.
Combine butter and remaining
6 ingredients in a saucepan;
cook over medium heat, stirring
constantly, until butter melts.
Pour over nuts, stirring to coat.
Bake for 20 minutes, stirring
once. Spread nuts on paper
towels to cool. Return nuts to
cans for storage.
Yield: 5 cups.

PERFECT COMBO

Smoky Chipotle Butter adds a burst of flavor to these warm and cheesy biscuits. A tin container lined with a napkin and filled with biscuits makes a rustic presentation.

CHEESE BISCUITS WITH CHIPOTLE BUTTER

1	(6.25-ounce) package biscuit mix
1	(6-ounce) package cornbread mix
1	(8-ounce) container sour cream
⅓	cup buttermilk
1	cup (4 ounces) shredded Cheddar cheese
1	teaspoon fajita seasoning

Chipotle Butter

Preheat oven to 400 degrees.
Stir together first 6 ingredients. Pat or roll dough to 1-inch thickness on a lightly floured surface. Cut with a 2-inch round cutter, and place rounds on a lightly greased baking sheet. Bake for 10 to 12 minutes. Serve with Chipotle Butter.
Yield: 20 biscuits.

Chipotle Butter

1	cup butter, softened
4	teaspoons chopped fresh parsley
2	chipotle peppers in adobo sauce, diced
4	teaspoons adobo sauce

Stir together all ingredients. Store in refrigerator up to a week.
Yield: 1 cup.

DELIGHTFUL LITTLE BITES

*I*t's hard to eat just one of these no-bake favorites made from orange juice concentrate and coconut combined with vanilla wafers and pecans. Wrap them by the dozen in clever little paper cones, and you'll have enough for five fast gifts.

ORANGE-NUT BALLS

½ cup butter or margarine, melted
1   (16-ounce) package powdered sugar, sifted
1   (6-ounce) can frozen orange juice concentrate, thawed
1   (12-ounce) package vanilla wafers, crushed
1   cup finely chopped pecans
1   (14-ounce) package sweetened flaked coconut

Stir together butter and sugar; stir in orange juice concentrate, vanilla wafers, and pecans. Shape into 1-inch balls, and roll in coconut. Cover and chill at least 1 hour or until firm. Store in refrigerator up to 3 weeks.
Yield: 5 dozen.

Christmas Cones
Twist square sheets of sturdy decorative paper into cone shapes. Secure them with glue, and tie them with ribbon and cording for a great presentation.

CHRISTMAS MIX

*R*ed cinnamon candies dropped into each cup of cider make for a spicy-sweet treat with every sip. Give a little bag of the candies along with the mix and a recipe card.

SPICED CIDER MIX

1	cup orange breakfast drink mix
1	cup sugar
1	cup lemonade iced tea mix
½	teaspoon ground cinnamon
¼	teaspoon ground cloves
¼	teaspoon ground allspice

Red cinnamon candies

Combine first 6 ingredients together in a large bowl, stirring well. Store in an airtight container. *Yield:* 3 cups.

Directions for recipe card: Combine 3 tablespoons Spiced Cider Mix, 1 teaspoon red cinnamon candies, and 1 cup boiling water. Stir well.

PIZZA SAUCE DIP KIT

The flavors of onion, garlic, and Italian seasoning combine to create a rich sauce that's great as a pizza spread or dipping sauce. Pour the sauce into a decorative jar, and package with some breadsticks.

PIZZA SAUCE

1	large onion, chopped
4	garlic cloves, minced
2	tablespoons olive oil
1	(28-ounce) can diced tomatoes, undrained
1	tablespoon dried Italian seasoning
1	teaspoon salt
½	teaspoon pepper

Sauté onion and garlic in hot oil in a large skillet over medium heat 10 minutes or until tender. Process tomatoes in blender or food processor until smooth; stir into onion mixture. Add Italian seasoning, salt, and pepper; bring to a boil. Reduce heat; simmer 1 hour, stirring occasionally. Cool. Process in a blender until smooth. Store in refrigerator.
Yield: 3 cups.

SWEET CINNAMON

Three ingredients are all that it takes to whip up a quick holiday gift. Pour this aromatic dessert sauce into a decorative container, and deliver with a purchased pound cake.

AMARETTO-CINNAMON SAUCE

¾ cup amaretto
¾ cup honey
¼ teaspoon ground
     cinnamon

Combine all ingredients in a small saucepan; cook over medium heat until mixture is thoroughly heated, stirring often.

Remove from heat, and cool to room temperature. Store in refrigerator.
Yield: 1⅓ cups.

BUNDLE OF BREAD

The predominant flavor of this traditional holiday bread comes from cardamom. Whole cardamom is much more fragrant than ground cardamom, but if the whole form isn't available, you can use 1 to 2 teaspoons ground cardamom.

NORWEGIAN CHRISTMAS BREAD

Whole cardamom pods
1	(¼-ounce) envelope active dry yeast
¼	cup warm water (100 to 110 degrees)
9	to 9¼ cups all-purpose flour, divided
1	cup sugar
2	cups milk
1	cup butter or margarine, melted
1	teaspoon salt
3	large eggs, beaten
1½	cups golden raisins
½	cup chopped red or green candied cherries
½	cup chopped red or green candied pineapple
½	cup coarsely chopped pecans

Place whole cardamom pods in a mortar; use a pestle to crack pods open. Discard pod fragments from the brown or black seeds, and crush seeds with pestle to equal 2 teaspoons. Set aside.

Combine yeast and warm water in a 1-cup glass measuring cup; let stand 5 minutes.

Combine yeast mixture, 2 cups flour, and next 4 ingredients in a large mixing bowl; beat at medium speed with an electric mixer 2 minutes. Beat in cardamom and eggs. Stir in fruit and pecans. Gradually stir in enough of remaining 7¼ cups flour to make a soft dough.

Turn dough out onto a well-floured surface, and knead until smooth and elastic (about 10 minutes). Place in a well-greased bowl, turning to grease top.

Cover and let rise in a warm place (85 degrees), free from drafts, 1 hour and 15 minutes or until doubled in bulk.

Punch dough down, and divide in half; roll 1 portion of dough into a 14- x 7-inch rectangle. Roll up dough, starting at short end, pressing firmly to eliminate air pockets; pinch ends to seal. Place dough, seam side down, in a well-greased 9- x 5-inch loafpan. Repeat procedure with remaining portion of dough.

Preheat oven to 350 degrees.

Cover and let rise in a warm place, free from drafts, 25 minutes or until doubled in bulk.

Bake for 30 minutes. Shield loaves with aluminum foil to prevent excessive browning. Bake for 20 more minutes or until

loaves sound hollow when tapped. Remove bread from pans immediately; cool on wire racks.
Yield: 2 loaves.

Tied with a Twist

Instead of wrapping a loaf of bread with a napkin or dish towel, consider using a bandanna. They come in all sorts of colors, and the corners tie together nicely. Wrap the loaf in plastic wrap first to keep it fresh. Tie on a gift tag for a personal touch.

BERRY DELICIOUS

Cranberries add a delicious zest to every bite of these shortbread treats. Glue a decorative button and ribbon to a corner of a napkin. Use the embellished napkin to line a basket, and arrange the cookies inside.

CRANBERRY BREAD COOKIES

½   cup shortening
½   cup butter, softened
2½   cups sugar, divided
2   large eggs
3   cups all-purpose flour
2   tablespoons grated orange
     rind
1   teaspoon baking powder
1   teaspoon salt
1   teaspoon cream of tartar
1½   cups chopped walnuts
1½   cups chopped fresh
     cranberries
¼   cup fresh orange juice
1   cup fresh cranberries

Beat ½ cup shortening and ½ cup butter at low speed with an electric mixer until fluffy; add 1½ cups sugar, beating until blended. Add eggs, 1 at a time, beating until blended after each addition.

Stir together flour and next 6 ingredients; add to butter mixture, beating at medium speed until blended. Add orange juice, beating until blended. Divide dough in half; cover and chill 8 hours.

Preheat oven to 350 degrees.

Work with 1 portion of dough at a time, keeping other chilled. Shape into 1-inch balls; roll balls in remaining 1 cup of sugar. (Dampen hands with water if dough is sticky.)

Place on greased baking sheets. Bake for 5 minutes. Press 1 cranberry into top of each cookie ball.

Bake for 7 to 8 more minutes or until edges begin to brown. Cool on baking sheets 1 minute. Remove to wire racks to cool.

Yield: 6½ dozen.

NUTTY NIBBLES

Friends will enjoy the taste of a holiday favorite in every bite of these delicious goodies. Pile them in a gift sack lined with a colorful holiday napkin, and add a Christmas tag made from craft foam. You can even make these cookies in November, as they can be frozen for up to a month.

PECAN PIE COOKIES

1	cup butter or margarine, softened
½	cup granulated sugar
½	cup dark corn syrup
2	large eggs, separated
2½	cups all-purpose flour
¼	cup butter or margarine
½	cup powdered sugar
3	tablespoons dark corn syrup
¾	cup finely chopped pecans

Beat 1 cup butter and granulated sugar at medium speed with an electric mixer until light and fluffy. Add ½ cup corn syrup and egg yolks, beating well. Gradually stir in flour; cover and chill 1 hour.

Melt ¼ cup butter in a heavy saucepan over medium heat; stir in powdered sugar and 3 tablespoons corn syrup. Cook, stirring often, until mixture boils. Remove from heat. Stir in pecans; chill 1 hour. Shape mixture by ½ teaspoonfuls into ½-inch balls; chill.

Preheat oven to 375 degrees.

Shape cookie dough into 1-inch balls; place 2 inches apart on lightly greased baking sheets. Beat egg whites until foamy. Brush egg whites on dough balls.

Bake for 5 minutes. Remove from oven, and press pecan balls into center of each cookie. Bake 8 to 10 more minutes or until lightly browned. Cool 2 minutes on baking sheets; remove to wire racks to cool completely. Freeze up to 1 month, if desired.
Yield: 4½ dozen.

JOYFUL JAR

*B*akers on your list will enjoy a jar of this ready-to-make cookie mix. All they'll need to do is add butter, an egg, and vanilla for a delicious batch of homemade treats.

OATMEAL-RAISIN-NUT COOKIE MIX IN A JAR

¾ cup firmly packed light brown sugar
½ cup granulated sugar
½ cup raisins
½ cup chopped pecans
1¾ cups uncooked regular oats
1 cup all-purpose flour
1 teaspoon baking soda
½ teaspoon salt

Layer first 5 ingredients in order given in a 1-quart wide-mouth jar. Firmly pack down each layer. Combine flour, soda, and salt. Layer flour mixture over oats in jar.

Directions for recipe card:
Preheat oven to 350 degrees. Empty cookie mix into a large mixing bowl; stir well. Add ¾ cup softened butter, 1 lightly beaten egg, and 1 teaspoon vanilla extract, stirring until completely blended. (You may need to finish mixing with your hands.) Shape into 1-inch balls. Place 2 inches apart on parchment-lined or lightly greased baking sheets. Bake for 13 to 14 minutes or until edges are lightly browned. Cool 1 minute on baking sheets. Remove cookies to wire racks to cool.
Yield: 4½ dozen.

PICKLES WITH PRESENTS

*B*read and Butter Pickles enhance just about any sandwich. These are wonderfully crisp and slightly sweet. Can jars of pickles in the summer for the ultimate make-ahead gift. Store them in a cool, dark place.

BREAD AND BUTTER PICKLES

6	pounds pickling cucumbers (about 20 cucumbers)
6	medium onions, sliced
2	medium-size green bell peppers, chopped
3	garlic cloves
⅓	cup pickling salt
Crushed ice	
5	cups sugar
3	cups cider vinegar (5% acidity)
2	tablespoons mustard seeds
1½	teaspoons ground turmeric
1½	teaspoons celery seeds

Wash cucumbers, and thinly slice. Combine cucumber, onion, and next 3 ingredients in a large Dutch oven. Cover with ice; mix thoroughly, and refrigerate 3 hours. Drain, removing ice.

Combine sugar and remaining ingredients; pour over cucumber mixture. Heat just until boiling. Remove garlic.

Pack hot mixture into hot jars, filling to ½ inch from top. Remove air bubbles; wipe jar rims. Cover at once with metal lids, and screw on bands. Process jars in boiling water bath 10 minutes.

Yield: 10 pints.

BEAN BAGS

If you're looking to make a big batch of gifts at once, try this soup mix. It makes enough to give to ten people. Package it by the 2-cupfuls in plastic bags first, and then place inside sheer fabric bags. Be sure to attach the Nine Bean-Chicken Soup recipe.

NINE BEAN SOUP MIX

1   (16-ounce) package barley
1   (16-ounce) package dried red beans
1   (16-ounce) package dried pinto beans
1   (16-ounce) package uncooked lentils
1   (16-ounce) package dried black-eyed peas
1   (16-ounce) package dried black beans
1   (16-ounce) package dried navy beans
1   (16-ounce) package dried great Northern beans
1   (16-ounce) package dried split peas

Combine all ingredients in a large bowl. Store in an airtight container.
Yield: 21 cups.

Nine Bean-Chicken Soup

2   cups Nine Bean Soup Mix
2   quarts water
2   cups chopped cooked chicken
1   large onion, chopped
1   garlic clove, minced
1   chicken bouillon cube
1   teaspoon salt
½   teaspoon pepper
1   (14½-ounce) can diced tomatoes
1   (10-ounce) can diced tomatoes and green chiles

Place Nine Bean Soup Mix in a Dutch oven; add water to cover, and let stand 30 minutes. Drain.
Bring soup mix, 2 quarts water, and next 6 ingredients to a boil in Dutch oven. Cover, reduce heat, and simmer 1 to 1½ hours.
Stir in diced tomatoes and tomatoes with chiles; return to a boil. Cover and simmer 30 minutes or until beans are tender, adding more water, if necessary.
Yield: 9 cups.

COFFEE BREAK

Orange rind adds a nice citrus flavor to this crunchy cookie that's perfect for dunking into a cup of coffee. A busy friend will enjoy relaxing with a mug of coffee and some biscotti.

ORANGE-PECAN BISCOTTI

4	large eggs
1	cup sugar
1½	tablespoons grated orange rind
2	tablespoons vegetable oil
1	teaspoon vanilla extract
1	teaspoon almond extract
3⅓	cups all-purpose flour
2	teaspoons baking powder
⅛	teaspoon salt
1	cup chopped pecans

Beat eggs and sugar at high speed with an electric mixer 5 minutes or until foamy. Add orange rind, oil, and extracts, beating until blended.

Combine flour, baking powder, and salt; add to sugar mixture, beating well. Fold in pecans. Cover and freeze 30 minutes or until firm.

Preheat oven to 325 degrees.

Divide dough in half; shape each portion into a 10- x 3½-inch log on a lightly greased baking sheet.

Bake for 25 minutes or until firm. Cool on baking sheets 5 minutes. Remove to wire racks to cool.

Cut each log diagonally into ½-inch slices with a serrated knife. Place on greased baking sheets. Bake for 15 minutes. Turn cookies over, and bake for 15 more minutes. Remove cookies to wire racks to cool.

Yield: 3¼ dozen.

PACKAGED IN A PAN

*R*efrigerated piecrusts form the base of these bite-size treats and make them easy as pie to make. Bake them in your own miniature muffin pans, and then remove them to cool on wire racks. For gift-giving, place them in new muffin pans, wrap with cellophane, and attach a pretty bow.

SPINACH QUICHES

1½ (15-ounce) packages refrigerated piecrusts
2 tablespoons butter or margarine
1 small onion, chopped
2 green onions, chopped
¼ cup chopped fresh parsley
1 (10-ounce) package frozen chopped spinach, thawed and well drained
1 tablespoon Worcestershire sauce
1 teaspoon salt
½ teaspoon pepper
3 large eggs
¼ cup milk
1½ cups (6 ounces) shredded Swiss cheese

Preheat oven to 350 degrees.

Cut 36 rounds from 3 piecrusts using a 2½-inch cutter. Press each circle into lightly greased miniature muffin pans.

Melt butter in a large skillet over medium heat. Add onions and parsley; sauté until onions are tender. Add spinach; cook 1 minute. Stir in Worcestershire sauce, salt, and pepper. Remove from heat.

Whisk together eggs and milk until blended; stir in cheese. Stir egg mixture into spinach mixture; spoon evenly into prepared pans.

Bake for 35 to 37 minutes. Remove immediately from pans, and cool on wire racks. Freeze quiches up to 2 months.
Yield: 3 dozen.

Directions for recipe card: Thaw frozen quiches overnight in refrigerator. Bake, uncovered, at 300 degrees for 10 minutes or until thoroughly heated.

FRUIT PIES

Juicy pears and dried cherries bubble inside a crispy dough crust. Present them in a napkin-lined basket or gift sack for a hearty afternoon snack or an anytime dessert.

DRIED CHERRY-AND-PEAR FRIED PIES

3   large pears, peeled and
    chopped
1   (6-ounce) package dried
    cherries
½   cup sugar
1   (15-ounce) package
    refrigerated piecrusts
Vegetable oil

Cook first 3 ingredients in a saucepan over medium heat 5 minutes. Reduce heat, and simmer, stirring occasionally, 10 minutes or until pears are tender. Chill 1 hour. Drain pear mixture, discarding liquid.

Roll piecrusts into 12-inch circles; cut each into 7 (4-inch) circles.

Spoon 1 rounded tablespoonful pear mixture onto half of each pastry circle. Moisten edges with water; fold dough over fruit mixture, pressing edges to seal. Crimp with a fork dipped in flour.

Pour oil to depth of ½ inch into a large heavy skillet; heat to 350 degrees.

Fry pies, in batches, 3 minutes on each side or until golden. Drain on paper towels. Serve any leftover fruit filling on toast or biscuits.

Yield: 14 pies.

Note: Pies may be baked on lightly greased baking sheets at 425 degrees for 12 minutes.

SAY CHEESE

A little hot jalapeño jelly really kicks up the flavor of this sharp Cheddar cheese spread. Pack it into little jars for gift giving. We guarantee it won't last long!

ZIPPY CHEESE SPREAD

2   cups (8 ounces) shredded
        sharp Cheddar cheese
1   bunch green onions,
        chopped (about 1 cup)
½   cup chopped pecans,
        toasted
2   tablespoons jalapeño
        pepper jelly
1   tablespoon mayonnaise

Combine all ingredients, stirring well. Serve immediately, or cover and chill. Serve with crackers. *Yield:* 2 cups.

Note: Shred your own cheese for this recipe rather than purchasing preshredded to make sure the spread is nice and moist.

PLATE OF CAKE

Carrot cake claims a new shape in this jellyroll with a lavish cream cheese frosting rolled up inside. This recipe makes two cake rolls—perfect for a couple of friends.

CARROT CAKE ROULAGE

4   large eggs
½   cup water
1   (18.25-ounce) package spice cake mix (we tested with Duncan Hines)
1   cup grated carrot
3   tablespoons powdered sugar, divided
1   (20-ounce) can crushed pineapple in heavy syrup
2   (16-ounce) containers ready-to-serve cream cheese frosting
½   cup chopped pecans, toasted
Powdered sugar

Preheat oven to 350 degrees. Coat 2 15- x 10-inch jellyroll pans with cooking spray. Line pans with wax paper; coat paper with cooking spray. Set aside.

Beat eggs at medium-high speed with a heavy-duty electric mixer 5 minutes. Add water, beating at low speed until blended. Gradually add cake mix, beating at low speed until moistened. Beat mixture at medium-high speed 2 minutes. Fold in grated carrot.

Spread batter evenly in prepared pans (layers will be thin). Bake 1 at a time on the middle rack 13 minutes or until each cake springs back when lightly touched in center.

Sift 1½ tablespoons powdered sugar in a 15- x 10-inch rectangle on a cloth towel; repeat with remaining sugar and a second towel. When cakes are done, immediately loosen from sides of pan; turn each out onto a sugared towel. Peel off wax paper. Starting at narrow end, tightly roll up each cake and towel together; place seam side down on wire racks to cool completely.

Drain pineapple, reserving ¼ cup syrup. Press pineapple between paper towels to remove excess moisture. Combine pineapple, cream cheese frosting, and ½ cup pecans; stir well.

Unroll cakes; brush each lightly with 2 tablespoons reserved pineapple syrup. Spread each cake with half of frosting mixture. Reroll cakes without towels; place seam side down on serving plates. Dust with powdered sugar.

Cover and chill at least 1 hour or up to 2 days.
Yield: 2 cake rolls.

Painted Plates
Transform plain plates into holiday pottery by painting the rims using ceramic paints. Designs in red and green such as dots, stars, and stripes are easy to create.

CHEERY LITTLE CREAM SAUCE

This rich sauce makes a delicious addition to chicken, pork, or veal. Package it in a little jar sealed with a strip of holiday stickers.

GREEN PEPPERCORN CREAM SAUCE

6	tablespoons butter or margarine
2	tablespoons minced shallots
1	tablespoon all-purpose flour
1	cup heavy whipping cream
¼	cup brandy
1	tablespoon green peppercorns, drained
¼	teaspoon salt
⅛	teaspoon pepper

Melt butter in a large skillet over medium heat; add shallots, and sauté 2 minutes. Stir in flour. Stir in cream, and cook until slightly thickened (do not boil). Stir in brandy, and cook 2 minutes. Stir in peppercorns, salt, and pepper. Cover and chill up to 3 days. Serve warm over chicken, pork, or veal. *Yield:* 1½ cups.

TASSELED TERRIFIC

Mediterranean flavors prevail in this easy eggplant dip. Shop at an Asian market for the five-spice powder. It's the ingredient that gives this recipe a real depth of flavor. Pour the dip into a clamp-top jar, tie on pretty tassels, and add some pita chips.

EGGPLANT AND WALNUT DIP

2	small eggplants, cut in half lengthwise (about ¾ pound each)
1	cup chopped, toasted walnuts, divided
¾	teaspoon Chinese five-spice powder
½	teaspoon salt
2	tablespoons half-and-half
¼	cup plain low-fat yogurt

Preheat oven to 425 degrees. Place eggplant, cut sides down, in a well-greased 13- x 9-inch pan. Bake for 30 minutes or until very tender. Cool. Peel and coarsely chop eggplant. Place eggplant in a food processor; add ½ cup walnuts and next 4 ingredients. Process until smooth. Spoon eggplant mixture into a bowl, and stir in remaining ½ cup walnuts. Cover and chill up to 2 days. Serve with pumpernickel slices or pita chips. *Yield:* 2⅔ cups.

DO THE CONGO

Everyone likes an easy bar cookie recipe that gets rave reviews. This is one of them. Wrap ribbon around a vegetable basket handle, line with burlap, and stack the bars inside.

CONGO BARS

2	cups firmly packed brown sugar
½	cup butter or margarine, melted
3	large eggs, lightly beaten
1	teaspoon vanilla extract
1½	cups all-purpose flour
1	cup chocolate graham cracker crumbs (about 6 whole crackers)
2	teaspoons baking powder
1	cup salted cashews, chopped
1	(11.5-ounce) package semisweet chocolate chunks or mega-morsels

Preheat oven to 350 degrees. Stir together first 4 ingredients. Combine flour, graham cracker crumbs, and baking powder; add to butter mixture, stirring well. Stir in cashews and chocolate chunks. (Batter will be thick.) Spread batter into a greased 13- x 9-inch pan; press gently into pan. Bake for 27 to 30 minutes. Cool completely in pan on a wire rack. Cut into bars. *Yield: 2 dozen.*

ON A ROLL

For a chocolaty gift, you can't beat these yummy rolls. Try this tip for glazing them: Simply place the glaze in a heavy-duty zip-top freezer bag, and seal securely. Then snip off one tiny corner of the bag, and pipe the glaze over the rolls. Deliver them in a decorative gift basket.

CHOCOLATE CINNAMON ROLLS

1	(¼-ounce) envelope active dry yeast
¾	cup warm water (100 to 110 degrees)
¼	cup butter or margarine, melted
1	teaspoon salt
¼	cup granulated sugar
1	large egg
⅓	cup cocoa
2¼	cups all-purpose flour, divided
1	tablespoon butter or margarine, softened
1½	teaspoons ground cinnamon
3	tablespoons granulated sugar
½	cup chopped pecans
2	cups sifted powdered sugar
2½	tablespoons milk

Combine yeast and warm water in a 2-cup glass measuring cup; let stand 5 minutes.

Combine yeast mixture, ¼ cup melted butter, salt, ¼ cup sugar, egg, cocoa, and 1 cup flour in a large mixing bowl; beat at medium speed with an electric mixer until well blended. Gradually stir in enough remaining flour to make a soft dough.

Turn dough out onto a well-floured surface, and knead until smooth and elastic (about 5 minutes). Place in a well-greased bowl, turning to grease top.

Cover and let rise in a warm place (85 degrees), free from drafts, 1 hour or until doubled in bulk.

Preheat oven to 425 degrees.

Punch dough down; turn out onto a lightly floured surface. Roll dough into a 12- x 9-inch rectangle; spread 1 tablespoon softened butter over dough. Combine cinnamon and 3 tablespoons sugar; sprinkle over butter. Sprinkle pecans over cinnamon mixture. Roll up dough, starting at short side, pressing firmly to eliminate air pockets; pinch seams to seal. Slice dough into 9 rolls; place rolls on a greased baking sheet. Cover; let rise in a warm place, free from drafts, 30 minutes or until doubled in bulk. Bake for 8 minutes or until golden.

Meanwhile, combine powdered sugar and milk, stirring until blended. Drizzle hot rolls with powdered sugar glaze.
Yield: 9 large rolls.

BREAKFAST IN A BASKET

Canned biscuits provide the base for this hearty little muffin that combines the rich flavors of egg, bacon, and two types of cheeses. Deliver them chilled in a napkin-lined basket, and be sure to include reheating instructions.

GOOD MORNING MUFFINS

2   green onions, chopped, divided

8   bacon slices, cooked and crumbled, divided

1   large egg

2   (3-ounce) packages cream cheese, softened

2   tablespoons milk

1   teaspoon garlic powder

½   cup (2 ounces) shredded Swiss cheese

1   (12-ounce) can refrigerated flaky biscuits (we tested with Hungry Jack Golden Layers biscuits)

Preheat oven to 375 degrees.
Reserve ¼ cup each chopped green onions and crumbled bacon.

Whisk together egg and next 3 ingredients. Whisk in Swiss cheese and remaining green onions.

Pat biscuits into 5-inch circles. Press biscuits into bottom and up sides of 10 muffin cups, forming a ¼-inch edge. Sprinkle bacon evenly in bottom of crusts. Pour cream cheese mixture evenly into crusts. Bake for 15 minutes or until set. Sprinkle with reserved ¼ cup bacon and chopped green onions. *Yield:* 10 muffins.

Directions for recipe card: Chill until ready to reheat. To reheat, place on a baking sheet; bake at 350 degrees for 10 minutes or until thoroughly heated.

TUTTI FRUTTI

This sassy salsa can play two delicious roles. Serve it as a salsa over grilled fish, chicken, or pork. It also works as a condiment spooned over cream cheese and served with cinnamon-flavored crisps or crackers. For the best texture and prettiest appearance, chop the ingredients by hand. Pour the salsa into a pretty jar; add a ribbon, label, and serving instructions.

FRESH FRUIT SALSA

1	medium-size orange, peeled, sectioned, and finely chopped
2	large kiwifruit, peeled and finely chopped
1	ripe peach, peeled and finely chopped
½	cup finely chopped fresh pineapple
¼	cup thinly sliced green onions
¼	cup finely chopped green bell pepper
1	jalapeño pepper, seeded and finely chopped
1	tablespoon fresh lime juice
1	cup fresh strawberries, quartered

Combine all ingredients in a large bowl; toss gently. Cover and chill at least 4 hours.
Yield: 2½ cups.

HEAVENLY TREATS

Chocolate mint wafer candies tucked into each cookie make for a sweet surprise with every bite.

STARLIGHT MINT SURPRISES

1	cup butter, softened
1	cup granulated sugar
½	cup firmly packed brown sugar
2	large eggs
1	teaspoon vanilla extract
3	cups all-purpose flour
1	teaspoon baking soda
½	teaspoon salt
2	(4.67-ounce) packages chocolate mints (we tested with Andes)

Preheat oven to 375 degrees. Beat butter at medium speed with an electric mixer until creamy; gradually add sugars, beating well. Add eggs, 1 at a time, beating until blended after each addition. Stir in vanilla.

Combine flour, soda, and salt; add to butter mixture, beating well.

Drop dough by teaspoonfuls 2 inches apart onto ungreased baking sheets. Press 1 candy on top of each mound of dough; cover with 1 teaspoonful dough. Bake for 9 minutes or until golden. Immediately remove to wire racks to cool.
Yield: 3 dozen.

Christmas Card Box

Create a gift box using old Christmas cards. Simply punch pairs of holes on three sides of four cards, and use ribbons to tie them together into a box shape. Put a card at the bottom of the box, punch pairs of holes in all four sides, and tie it to the box with ribbon. Fill the box with tissue, and add a gift tag.

PEPPERMINT TWIST

This make-ahead dessert, rich in chocolate and peppermint, just melts in your mouth. Decorate a white bakery box with peppermints, red and white ribbon, and a red and white gift tag that hints at the flavors inside.

FUDGY CHOCOLATE MALT-PEPPERMINT PIE

½   cup butter or margarine
2   (1-ounce) unsweetened chocolate baking squares
1   (1-ounce) semisweet chocolate baking square
1   cup granulated sugar
2   large eggs
1   teaspoon vanilla extract
¼   cup all-purpose flour
¼   cup chocolate malt mix (we tested with Ovaltine Chocolate Malt mix)
¼   teaspoon salt
¼   teaspoon ground cinnamon
1   cup coarsely chopped pecans
1   pint peppermint ice cream, softened
1   cup whipping cream
¼   cup powdered sugar
¼   cup crushed peppermint candy

Preheat oven to 325 degrees.
Melt first 3 ingredients in a heavy saucepan over low heat, stirring occasionally until smooth. Remove from heat; cool.

Beat chocolate mixture and 1 cup sugar at medium speed with an electric mixer until blended. Add eggs and vanilla, beating until smooth. Add flour and next 3 ingredients, beating until blended. Stir in pecans. Pour into a lightly greased 9-inch pieplate.

Bake for 40 minutes. Remove from oven; cool completely on a wire rack.

Press down center of crust gently. Spread ice cream over crust. Cover and freeze 8 hours.

Beat whipping cream and powdered sugar at medium speed with electric mixer until soft peaks form. Spread over ice cream. Sprinkle with crushed candy. Cover and freeze up to 1 month. Let stand at room temperature 15 minutes before slicing.

Yield: 1 (9-inch) pie.

BOTTLED FLAVOR

Friends will enjoy this liqueur splashed in hot coffee drinks or over ice cream. Pour it into a decorative bottle wrapped with mesh fabric and adorned with ribbon and little ornaments.

COFFEE LIQUEUR

5	cups sugar
1	(2-ounce) jar instant coffee granules
4	cups boiling water
1	(1-liter) bottle vodka
1	vanilla bean, split lengthwise

Combine sugar and coffee granules in a large metal or glass bowl; add boiling water, stirring until sugar and coffee granules dissolve. Cool to room temperature. Stir in vodka. Pour into 3 (1-quart) jars or decorative bottles.

Cut vanilla bean into thirds; place 1 piece in each jar or bottle. Cover and let stand at room temperature at least 12 days before serving.
Yield: 10 cups.

Directions for recipe card: Use in recipes calling for coffee-flavored liqueur, or simply enjoy in hot coffee drinks or over ice cream.

GIVE IT A SWIRL

Paint gold dots around the edge of a simple glass plate— this two-toned cake needs no other adornment.

THE BEST MARBLE CAKE

1	cup shortening
3	cups sugar
6	large eggs
3	cups sifted cake flour
½	teaspoon baking soda
½	teaspoon salt
1	cup buttermilk
1	teaspoon vanilla extract
½	cup chocolate syrup

Preheat oven to 350 degrees.

Beat shortening at medium speed with an electric mixer about 2 minutes or until fluffy. Gradually add sugar, beating 5 to 7 minutes. Add eggs, 1 at a time, beating just until yellow disappears.

Combine flour, soda, and salt; add to shortening mixture alternately with buttermilk, beginning and ending with flour mixture. Beat at low speed just until blended after each addition. Stir in vanilla. Pour half of batter into a greased and floured 10-inch tube pan. Add chocolate syrup to remaining half of batter. Spoon chocolate batter over plain batter. Swirl batter gently with a knife.

Bake for 1 hour or until a long wooden pick inserted in center of cake comes out clean. Cool in pan on a wire rack 10 to 15 minutes; remove from pan, and cool completely on wire rack.

Yield: 1 (10-inch) cake.

The Best
Marble Cake

BRIGHT IDEA

Break away from the usual red and green, and opt for bright, cheerful colors when packaging these squares that boast the pairing of peanut butter and chocolate. Crushed graham cracker complements the classic combination with a satisfying crunch.

PEANUT BUTTER SQUARES

4	cups sifted powdered sugar
1	(5⅓-ounce) package graham crackers, crushed (about 1⅔ cups)
1	cup creamy peanut butter
1	cup butter or margarine, melted
1	cup semisweet chocolate morsels, melted

Stir together first 4 ingredients in a medium bowl. Firmly press mixture into an ungreased 13- x 9-inch pan. Spread melted chocolate evenly over cracker layer.

Let cool on a wire rack at room temperature. Cover and chill at least 2 hours. Cut into squares. *Yield:* 2 dozen.

Fantastic Foam

A flowery, fun theme is easy to achieve with colored craft foam. To make this wrap, cover the base of an oval wooden box with self-adhesive striped foam, leaving enough space for the box lid to fit securely on the base. Cover the top of the lid with self-adhesive foam. Glue grosgrain ribbon around the rim of the lid. Glue precut foam flowers to ribbon. Attach foam circles to flowers. You can also make your own foam flowers, if desired.

CHRISTMAS CRUNCH

A buttery toasted crunch awaits inside these white candy clusters. Give them in a box dressed up with bead trim, matching ribbon, and a gift tag.

CRUNCHY VANILLA CLUSTERS

1	(3-ounce) package ramen noodles
¾	cup pecan pieces
½	cup sliced almonds
2	tablespoons butter or margarine, melted
1	(12-ounce) package white chocolate or vanilla morsels (we tested with Nestlé)

Gently crush ramen noodles before opening package. Open package and discard flavoring packet. Sauté crushed noodles, pecans, and almonds in butter in a large skillet over medium heat until toasted. (Be careful not to crush noodles too finely while sautéing.) Pour noodle mixture into a large bowl to cool.

Melt white chocolate morsels according to package directions. Pour melted chocolate over cooled noodle mixture, tossing gently to coat. Drop candy mixture by rounded tablespoonfuls onto wax paper; let stand until firm (about 45 minutes). Store clusters in an airtight container at room temperature.

Yield: about 2 dozen.

Note: It's important to melt white chocolate morsels according to package directions. If heated too quickly or at too high a temperature, the morsels will not melt properly. We recommend using microwave directions for melting.

SANTA'S SAUCE

*M*ayonnaise provides the "white" in this North Carolina-style sauce that's tangy with vinegar and pumped up with pepper. Best of all, this make-ahead favorite takes just five minutes to make. Package it in a plastic container tied with cording and embellished with festive trinkets. Wrap cording around a small brush to complete the set. On the gift card, make a serving suggestion to use to baste chicken during grilling.

WHITE CHRISTMAS BARBECUE SAUCE

1½	cups mayonnaise
⅓	cup cider vinegar
¼	cup lemon juice
2	tablespoons sugar
2	tablespoons cracked pepper
2	tablespoons white wine Worcestershire sauce

Combine all ingredients in a small bowl; stir with a wire whisk. Cover and chill.
Yield: 2¼ cups.

APPLE APPEAL

Nothing identifies Lowcountry cooking more than its extensive use of condiments, particularly homemade ones. This easy-to-make stove-top chutney can be prepared in about an hour. Put this tangy make-ahead gift into an acrylic container and tie on a spreader with raffia and beads.

APPLE CHUTNEY

13	cups chopped peeled Granny Smith or other tart apple (about 4 pounds)
3	cups chopped onion (about 1 pound)
2	cups raisins
2	cups packed brown sugar
2	cups cider vinegar
¼	cup finely chopped seeded jalapeño pepper
1	teaspoon mustard seeds

Combine all ingredients in a large nonaluminum Dutch oven or stockpot. Bring to a boil. Reduce heat; simmer 45 minutes or until most of liquid evaporates. *Yield:* 9½ cups (serving size: ¼ cup).

Note: Store chutney in an airtight container in refrigerator for up to 2 weeks.

HOLIDAY FIESTA

Help a friend add some heat to a cold winter night with a gift from the Southwest. This recipe makes two pretty braided loaves, so keep one for yourself or share with two friends.

JALAPEÑO-CHEESE BRAIDS

5 cups bread flour, divided
2 (¼-ounce) envelopes active dry yeast
2 teaspoons sugar
1 teaspoon salt
1 cup water
1 cup milk
3 tablespoons butter
1 large egg
1¼ cups (5 ounces) shredded sharp Cheddar cheese, divided
1 cup sliced pickled jalapeño peppers, drained and divided
¾ cup (3 ounces) sharp Cheddar cheese, cubed
¼ cup butter or margarine, melted

Combine 2 cups flour, yeast, sugar, and salt in a large mixing bowl.

Combine water, milk, and 3 tablespoons butter in a saucepan; heat until butter melts. Remove from heat, and cool to 120 to 130 degrees. Gradually add hot liquids to flour mixture, beating at medium speed with an electric mixer. Beat 2 minutes. Add egg; beat 1 minute. Stir in 1 cup shredded cheese and ¾ cup peppers. Using a wooden spoon, gradually stir in enough remaining flour to make a soft dough.

Turn dough out onto a well-floured surface; add cubed cheese, and knead dough until smooth and elastic (about 8 minutes). Place in a well-greased bowl, turning to grease top.

Cover and let rise in a warm place (85 degrees), free from drafts, 40 minutes or until doubled in bulk. Punch dough down; divide in half. Shape each portion into 3 ropes; place ropes on a lightly greased large baking sheet. (You can bake loaves on 1 large baking sheet or on 2 smaller pans, if necessary.) Braid ropes, pinching ends under. Place remaining ¼ cup peppers between ropes. Cover and let rise in a warm place 20 minutes or until doubled in bulk. Brush loaves gently with melted butter. Sprinkle with remaining ¼ cup cheese.

Preheat oven to 375 degrees.

Bake for 20 to 22 minutes or until golden. Remove from pan immediately. Cool on wire racks. *Yield:* 2 loaves.

Magical Mats

Make swirls around the rims of straw place mats using puff paint. Let the paint dry completely. Add a matching bandanna or napkin, place your gift inside, and seal with a matching ribbon.

DRIZZLE DAZZLE

*E*njoy a rich cream cheese mixture with every bite of this sweet bread
drizzled with a powdered sugar glaze. This make-ahead recipe makes two gifts.

Merry Christmas

CREAM CHEESE BRAIDS

1 (16-ounce) package hot
  roll mix
1 (8-ounce) package cream
  cheese, softened
⅓ cup granulated sugar
1 teaspoon vanilla extract
1 egg yolk
Pinch of salt
1 egg yolk, lightly beaten
1 cup sifted powdered sugar
1½ tablespoons milk
1 teaspoon vanilla extract

Prepare dough from hot roll mix
according to package directions
using yeast packet. Turn dough
out onto a lightly floured surface,
and knead 4 or 5 times. Divide
dough in half. Roll each portion
into a 12- x 8-inch rectangle.
Carefully place each on a greased
baking sheet.

Beat cream cheese and next 4
ingredients at medium speed with
an electric mixer until blended.

Spread half of mixture lengthwise
down center of each rectangle.

Cut 9 (3-inch-deep) slits into
long sides of each rectangle. Fold
strips over cream cheese filling,
alternating sides and making a
braid. Pinch ends to seal, and tuck
under, if desired.

Cover and let rise in warm place
(85 degrees), free from drafts, 30
minutes. Brush tops with beaten
egg yolk.

Preheat oven to 375 degrees.
Bake for 15 minutes.

Stir together powdered sugar,
milk, and 1 teaspoon vanilla;
drizzle over warm loaves.
Yield: 2 loaves.

Note: Freeze baked braids, if
desired. Thaw in refrigerator, and
drizzle with glaze before giving.

Tray Terrific
Paint an unfinished wooden
tray with acrylic paint. (We
used green for the inside,
orange for the top rim, and
gold for the outside.) Let
dry. Coat several times with
a decoupage paste to add
luster and depth. Let dry.
Glue flat-back rhinestones to
top of rim. Thread an oval
gift tag and extra beads with
thin red cord to large silk
ribbon wrap.

MORNING MAGIC

*T*his syrup looks rich and tempting in a resealable glass jar with festive ribbon tied at the neck. Add colorful beads for extra charm.

MOCHA LATTE SYRUP

¾	cup sugar
⅓	cup unsweetened cocoa
¼	cup instant espresso or dark roast instant coffee
½	teaspoon ground cinnamon
½	cup water
2	tablespoons vanilla extract

Combine sugar and next 3 ingredients in a medium saucepan. Whisk in water, and bring to a boil over medium heat. Boil 1 minute, stirring often. Remove from heat; stir in 2 tablespoons vanilla extract. Refrigerate up to 2 weeks.
Yield: 1¼ cups.

Directions for recipe card: To prepare Mocha Latte Beverage, spoon 1 tablespoon Mocha Latte Syrup into a coffee cup; stir in ¾ cup hot milk.

PLATE OF PERFECTION

A wooden spoon will take you from start to finish with this recipe. The rum flavor permeates these petite cakes that can be frozen. A decoupaged plate lends flair to these sophisticated morsels, and a jingle bell and spiral shape make for a whimsical tag.

RUM FUDGE CAKES

1	cup butter
4	(1-ounce) unsweetened chocolate baking squares
4	(1-ounce) semisweet chocolate baking squares
1⅓	cups granulated sugar
1½	teaspoons rum extract
⅓	cup heavy whipping cream
3	large eggs
1	cup all-purpose flour
1	cup semisweet chocolate mini-morsels

Powdered sugar

Preheat oven to 375 degrees. Melt butter and 8 ounces chocolate in a heavy saucepan over medium-low heat, stirring often. Remove from heat, and cool completely. Stir in granulated sugar, rum extract, and whipping cream until blended. Add eggs, 1 at a time, stirring until blended after each addition. Gradually fold in flour. Stir in mini-morsels.

Spoon batter into lightly greased or paper-lined miniature (1¾-inch) muffin pans, filling almost full. Bake for 14 minutes or until a wooden pick inserted in center of cakes comes out clean. Remove from pans immediately, and cool on wire racks.

Sprinkle cakes with powdered sugar.
Yield: 4 dozen.

CRAN-ORANGE CRAVINGS

There's a zest of flavor in these breakfast favorites. Trim two sides of a napkin with beaded fringe, place it inside a basket, and tie on a gift tag and ornaments for a welcome holiday treat.

STREUSEL CRAN-ORANGE MUFFINS

1½	cups all-purpose flour
1	teaspoon baking powder
½	teaspoon baking soda
½	teaspoon salt
1	large egg, lightly beaten
½	cup cranberry-orange relish
1	teaspoon grated orange rind
⅓	cup freshly squeezed orange juice
¼	cup firmly packed brown sugar
¼	cup butter, melted
⅓	cup chopped pecans
¼	cup firmly packed brown sugar
½	teaspoon ground cinnamon

Preheat oven to 400 degrees.

Combine first 4 ingredients in a large mixing bowl; make a well in center of flour mixture.

Combine egg and next 5 ingredients; add to dry ingredients, stirring just until moistened. Spoon batter into greased muffin pans, filling two-thirds full.

Combine pecans and remaining 2 ingredients. Sprinkle batter with pecan mixture. Bake for 15 minutes or until golden. Remove from pans immediately, and cool on a wire rack.

Yield: 1 dozen.

CAN'T-MISS CANDY

Two ingredients are all it takes to make this sweet holiday treat that stacks equally well in gift bags or tins. Give colored gift bags Christmas flavor by gluing on fun holiday shapes—like snowflakes, trees, and candy canes.

PEPPERMINT CHRISTMAS CANDY

1   (24-ounce) package vanilla bark coating
10 peppermint candy canes, crushed (about 4 ounces) or 24 hard peppermint candies, crushed

Line a 15- x 10-inch jellyroll pan with wax paper; set aside.

Place vanilla coating in top of a double boiler; bring water to a boil. Reduce heat to low; cook until coating melts, stirring occasionally. Remove from heat; stir in crushed candy canes.

Spread mixture thinly and evenly in prepared pan. Cool completely; break into pieces.

Yield: 20 servings (1½ pounds).

POUNDS OF FLAVOR

*O*nce you taste these buttery gems, you'll agree that they're a hands-down winner for any occasion. Bundle them in cellophane and tie with a trinket. Place inside a decorative flowerpot that's sure to be enjoyed after all the cookies are gone.

POUND CAKE COOKIES

1	cup butter, softened
1	cup sugar
1	egg yolk
1	teaspoon rum or ½ teaspoon rum flavoring
½	teaspoon vanilla extract
2¼	cups sifted cake flour
½	teaspoon salt

About 42 pecan halves

Beat butter at medium speed with an electric mixer until creamy; gradually add sugar, beating well. Add egg yolk, rum, and vanilla; beat well. Combine flour and salt in a bowl; gradually add to butter mixture, beating well. Cover and chill at least 2 hours or until firm.

Preheat oven to 350 degrees.

Shape dough into 1-inch balls; place 2 inches apart on ungreased baking sheets. Press 1 pecan half into each cookie.

Bake for 11 to 12 minutes or until edges are lightly browned. Cool 2 minutes on baking sheets; remove to wire racks to cool completely.

Yield: about 3½ dozen.

TIED IN KNOTS

A refreshing orange glaze is the sweet secret behind these melt-in-your-mouth nibbles. Present them in a golden basket lined with a beaded napkin.

ORANGE KNOT ROLLS

5	cups bread flour, divided
2	(¼-ounce) envelopes rapid-rise yeast
⅓	cup sugar
2	tablespoons grated orange rind
1	teaspoon salt
½	cup orange juice
2	large eggs
1	cup warm milk (100 to 110 degrees)
½	cup butter, melted
	Orange Glaze

Combine 2 cups flour and next 4 ingredients in a large bowl. Add orange juice, eggs, warm milk, and melted butter, stirring to combine. Gradually stir in enough of remaining flour to make a soft dough.

Turn dough onto a lightly floured surface, and knead until smooth and elastic (about 8 minutes). Place in a well-greased bowl, turning to grease top.

Cover and let rise in a warm place (85 degrees), free from drafts, 30 minutes or until doubled in bulk.

Punch dough down; turn out onto a lightly floured surface. Roll dough into a 16- x 10-inch rectangle. Cut dough into 1-inch strips. Shape each strip into a knot, tucking ends under. Place rolls on large lightly greased baking sheets. Cover and let rise in a warm place, free from drafts, 30 minutes or until doubled in bulk.

Preheat oven to 400 degrees.

Bake for 12 minutes or until lightly browned. Drizzle Orange Glaze over warm rolls.
Yield: 16 rolls.

Orange Glaze

2	cups sifted powdered sugar
¼	cup orange juice
2	teaspoons grated orange rind

Combine all ingredients in a small bowl; drizzle over cooked rolls.
Yield: 1 cup.

Note: Chill rolls on baking sheet while baking first pan of rolls. Chilling prevents rolls from over-proofing while first rolls bake.

Basket and Napkin Combo

To create a sparkling wrap, attach colorful beads to a gold wire basket. Then trim the edges of a sheer napkin with gold beads. Line the basket with a solid napkin topped with the sheer napkin.

PARTY IN A BAG

Pull out some pantry staples to make this crispy cereal mix. The microwave instructions cut cooking time to a minimum.

CURRIED PARTY MIX

¼   cup butter or margarine, melted
2   teaspoons curry powder
¾   to 1 teaspoon seasoned salt
½   teaspoon ground cumin
⅛   teaspoon ground red pepper
5   cups bite-size crispy corn cereal squares (we tested with Corn Chex)
2   cups small pretzels (not pretzel sticks)
1½   cups whole almonds
1½   cups salted peanuts

Preheat oven to 250 degrees. Combine first 5 ingredients in a small bowl. Combine cereal and remaining 3 ingredients in a large bowl. Stir butter mixture, and pour evenly over cereal mixture. Stir cereal mixture until coated.

Spread mixture in a greased roasting pan or 15- x 10-inch jellyroll pan. Bake for 1 hour, stirring every 15 minutes. Spread mixture in a single layer on paper towels; cool completely. Store in an airtight container.
Yield: 10 cups.

Microwave Directions: Melt butter in a large microwave-safe bowl at HIGH 55 seconds; stir in seasonings. Gradually add cereal, pretzels, and nuts; stir until well coated. Microwave at HIGH 5 to 6 minutes, stirring and scraping sides and bottom of bowl with a rubber spatula every 2 minutes. Spread mixture in a single layer on paper towels; cool completely.

TEA TIME

The flavors of citrus and cinnamon combine to create a refreshing holiday treat. Pour the mix into a bejeweled jar tied with a ribbon and a recipe card.

SPICED TEA PUNCH MIX

1	(21.1-ounce) jar instant orange breakfast drink mix
¾	cup instant tea with lemon
1½	cups sugar
1½	teaspoons ground cloves
1½	teaspoons ground cinnamon

Combine all ingredients in a large bowl; store in an airtight container.
Yield: 5 cups.

Directions for recipe card: Bring ¾ cup Spiced Tea Punch Mix, 1 (46-ounce) can unsweetened pineapple juice, 1 (46-ounce) can apple juice, and 2 cups water to a boil in a Dutch oven; reduce heat, and simmer, stirring occasionally, 15 minutes. Serve hot or cold.
Yield: 15 cups.

Bejeweled Jars
Put a drop of clear silicone on the flat side of a glass gem. Press it firmly against the glass jar in the desired position. Hold it in place for a few seconds to let the glue set. Let it dry for 24 hours.

LEMON DELIGHT

A lemony glaze sweetens these refreshingly tart cookie squares. Crown your gift box with a faux lemon to signal the tangy treat inside.

LEMON-COCONUT BAR COOKIES

Cookies:

1   cup all-purpose flour
2   tablespoons granulated sugar
¼   cup chilled butter, cut into small pieces
1   cup packed brown sugar
3   tablespoons fresh lemon juice
2   large eggs
½   cup sweetened flaked coconut

Glaze:

⅔   cup powdered sugar
1   teaspoon grated lemon rind
2   tablespoons fresh lemon juice

Preheat oven to 350 degrees. To prepare cookies, lightly spoon flour into a dry measuring cup; level with a knife. Combine flour and granulated sugar in a bowl; cut in butter with a pastry blender or fork until mixture resembles coarse meal.

Press mixture into a lightly greased 9-inch square baking pan. Bake for 10 minutes.

Combine brown sugar, 3 tablespoons juice, and eggs in a medium bowl, stirring with a whisk. Stir in coconut; pour evenly into pan. Bake 22 more minutes or until set.

To prepare glaze, combine powdered sugar, rind, and 2 tablespoons juice, stirring with a whisk. Spread glaze evenly over cookies. Cool completely in pan on a wire rack. Cut cookies into squares.

Yield: 16 servings.

Textured Top

Here's a great use for all of your leftover scraps of pretty paper. Take a large, shallow box and wrap the lid with rice paper. Layer rectangles of your favorite materials to place on lid. (We used parchment paper, copper screen, and silk-screened paper.) Attach layers to each other with glue and secure on lid with copper wire. Secure decorative fruit to lid with copper wire and curl ends and fruit stems. Tie on a ribbon and gift tag. Line sides of the lid with a strip of corrugated paper. Glue paper squares together and attach to front center of lid. Punch a hole through the center of the paper squares and lid. Thread copper wire through hole and attach bead.

THE ENVELOPE, PLEASE

*U*se scraps of wrapping paper to create little envelopes for this spicy seasoning. Seal the mix in plastic bags and place them inside the envelopes. Deliver each with the recipe instructions and a batch of taco shells.

TACO SEASONING MIX

2	teaspoons dried minced onion
1	teaspoon salt
1	teaspoon chili powder
½	teaspoon cornstarch
½	teaspoon instant minced garlic
½	teaspoon dried crushed red pepper
½	teaspoon ground cumin
¼	teaspoon dried oregano

Stir together all ingredients. Store in an airtight container up to 1 month.
Yield: 2 tablespoons.

Directions for recipe card:
To use for tacos, cook 1 pound ground beef in a large skillet, stirring until it crumbles and is no longer pink; drain. Stir in Taco Seasoning Mix and ½ cup water. Cook over medium heat 5 minutes or until liquid evaporates. Spoon meat mixture into taco shells.

CRANBERRY CHEER

Easy! This microwave cranberry sauce goes from kitchen to gift wrap in about 15 minutes.

CITRUS-SPIKED CRANBERRY SAUCE

1	pound fresh or frozen cranberries, thawed (4 cups)
1	to 1½ cups sugar
1	tablespoon grated orange rind
1	cup orange juice

Dash of salt

Combine all ingredients in a 2-quart microwaveable casserole. Cover with heavy-duty plastic wrap; fold back a small corner of wrap to allow steam to escape. Microwave at HIGH 15 minutes, stirring every 5 minutes, until cranberry skins pop. Let stand, covered, 5 minutes. Stir. Serve warm or chilled.
Yield: 2¾ cups.

Tulle Sacks

Tulle gift bags are easy to make by simply cutting a length of tulle and sewing or gluing each of the two sides together. They're great for decorating bottles but could also be used to hold other treats.

JAR FULL OF JELLY

Since grapefruit and cranberries are in season in winter, they make a refreshing Christmas treat. Deliver this marmalade made from the tangy duo in a glass canister embellished with colorful beads.

EASY GRAPEFRUIT-CRANBERRY MARMALADE

4   medium grapefruit (about 4 pounds)
1½   cups water
2½   cups fresh cranberries
3   cups sugar

Using a vegetable peeler, carefully remove rind from grapefruit; discard bitter white pith. Cut grapefruit rind into julienne strips. Peel and section grapefruit.

Combine grapefruit rind, sections, and water in a large saucepan; bring mixture to a boil. Reduce heat to medium, and simmer 15 minutes, stirring occasionally. Add cranberries, and cook 10 minutes. Stir in sugar; cook 35 minutes or until slightly thickened, stirring occasionally. Pour into jars or airtight containers. Store in refrigerator up to 3 weeks. *Yield:* 5¼ cups (serving size: 2 tablespoons).

COCONUT TREATS

*B*utterscotch morsels melt throughout these crisp cookies. Glue fringe around the edge of a basket and to a small gift tag. Line the basket with napkins to match, and pile the cookies inside.

COCONUT SCOTCHIES

½	cup butter or margarine, softened
½	cup granulated sugar
½	cup firmly packed brown sugar
2	large eggs
1	teaspoon vanilla extract
2	cups all-purpose flour
½	teaspoon baking soda
½	teaspoon salt
1	cup butterscotch morsels
½	cup chopped pecans
1½	cups flaked coconut

Preheat oven to 350 degrees.

Beat butter at medium speed with an electric mixer until creamy; gradually add sugars, beating well. Add eggs and vanilla; beat well.

Combine flour, soda, and salt; add to butter mixture, and beat well. Stir in butterscotch morsels and pecans.

Place flaked coconut in a shallow dish. Drop dough by rounded teaspoonfuls into coconut, rolling to coat dough with coconut while shaping dough into balls. Place balls on greased baking sheets. Bake for 10 minutes. Immediately remove to wire racks to cool. *Yield:* 4 dozen.

Coconut Scotchies

97

MERRY MAYONNAISE

*F*riends will enjoy spreading this tarragon-inspired mayonnaise over hard rolls with
sliced roast beef, on hamburgers, or on tomato sandwiches. Glue some decorative
paper and a button to the top of a jar and spoon the mayonnaise inside.
Tie on a gift tag with a smaller button to coordinate.

BÉARNAISE MAYONNAISE

⅓	cup dry white wine
1	tablespoon white wine vinegar
2	shallots, minced
1	cup mayonnaise
2	tablespoons chopped fresh tarragon
1	teaspoon grated lemon rind
⅛	teaspoon pepper

Cook wine, vinegar, and shallots in a small saucepan over medium-high heat 5 minutes or until liquid is reduced to 1 tablespoon. Remove from heat, and cool.

Stir together mayonnaise and remaining ingredients; stir in wine reduction. Cover and chill up to 7 days. Garnish, if desired. *Yield:* 1 cup.

Tomato-Basil Mayonnaise: Stir together 1 cup mayonnaise, 2 tablespoons tomato paste, and 2 tablespoons chopped fresh basil until blended.

Gremolata Mayonnaise: Stir together 1 cup mayonnaise; 2 tablespoons chopped fresh parsley; 2 tablespoons grated lemon rind; and 1 garlic clove, pressed.

Pistachio Topping adds crunch to this holiday quick bread. Cut cake into squares to fill a napkin-lined basket. Dabs of fabric paint decorate the napkin while pretty ribbon attaches the gift tag to the basket.

PUMPKIN-PISTACHIO BREAKFAST BREAD

1½	cups butter or margarine, softened
1½	cups granulated sugar
3	large eggs
3	cups all-purpose flour
2	teaspoons baking powder
½	teaspoon baking soda
¾	teaspoon salt
1	teaspoon ground cinnamon
½	teaspoon ground ginger
¼	teaspoon ground cloves
1½	cups canned pumpkin
1	cup raisins
1½	teaspoons vanilla extract

Pistachio Topping

½	(3-ounce) package cream cheese, softened
1	cup sifted powdered sugar
2	tablespoons milk

Preheat oven to 350 degrees.

Beat butter at medium speed with an electric mixer until creamy; gradually add 1½ cups granulated sugar, beating well. Add eggs, 1 at a time, beating until blended after each addition.

Combine flour and next 6 ingredients in a large bowl; add to butter mixture alternately with pumpkin, beginning and ending with flour mixture. Stir in raisins and vanilla.

Spread cake batter into a greased and floured 13- x 9-inch pan; sprinkle with Pistachio Topping.

Bake for 45 to 50 minutes or until a wooden pick inserted in center comes out clean. Cool on a wire rack.

Beat cream cheese, powdered sugar, and 2 tablespoons milk in a small bowl until smooth, using a wire whisk. Using whisk, drizzle cream cheese mixture over cake.

Yield: 12 servings.

Pistachio Topping

⅔	cup unsalted pistachio nuts
⅓	cup firmly packed light brown sugar
¼	cup all-purpose flour
½	teaspoon ground cinnamon
¼	teaspoon ground ginger
⅛	teaspoon ground cloves
2	tablespoons butter or margarine, cut into pieces

Process first 6 ingredients in a food processor until nuts are coarsely chopped. Add butter to processor; pulse until mixture is crumbly. Set aside.

Yield: 1 cup.

FESTIVELY FRESH

Lemon juice adds a bit of zest to this flavorful dressing. A small splash goes a long way. Pour the dressing in a glass bottle embellished with beads and wire. Add a small gift tag with a bit of wire.

LEMON-BASIL DRESSING

⅓	cup olive oil
¼	cup fresh lemon juice
¼	cup chopped fresh basil
2	garlic cloves, minced
1	teaspoon salt
½	teaspoon sugar
½	teaspoon dry mustard

Combine all ingredients, and stir well. Cover and chill. *Yield:* about 1 cup.

Great Gift Tags

Turn purchased price tags or round labels found at office supply stores into charming little gift tags. Simply write a message, remove the strings, and attach with wire or ribbon.

LOVE FROM THE OVEN

Ward off the cold weather by whipping up a batch of this sweet treat for a friend. Spoon this easy spread into a clamp-top jar and decorate with a richly-colored ribbon, a simple card, and an old-fashioned ornament.

OVEN APPLE BUTTER

8	Granny Smith apples, peeled and diced
1	cup apple juice
1	cup sugar
1	teaspoon ground cinnamon

Preheat oven to 275 degrees.

Cook diced apple and juice in a Dutch oven over medium heat 30 minutes or until apple is tender. Stir until apple is mashed. Stir in sugar and cinnamon. Pour apple mixture into a lightly greased 11- x 7-inch baking dish.

Bake for 3½ hours, stirring every hour, or until spreading consistency. Cover and chill. *Yield:* 2 cups.

Spiced Oven Apple Butter: Increase cinnamon to 2 teaspoons and add ½ teaspoon ground cloves and ¼ teaspoon ground allspice.

CHOCOLATE-FROSTED CHEER

Spoon canned frosting into a glass clamp-top jar to turn this home-baked bread into a chocolaty treat for a special friend. These loaves freeze well, so make them ahead. Thaw completely before tying them in ribbon.

CREAM CHEESE AND CHOCOLATE DANISH

½ cup water (100 to 110 degrees)
2 (¼-ounce) envelopes active dry yeast
½ cup milk
¼ cup butter or margarine, melted
4 to 5¼ cups all-purpose flour, divided
½ cup sugar
2 large eggs
1 teaspoon salt
1 (8-ounce) package cream cheese, softened
¼ cup sugar
1 egg yolk
Favorite chocolate frosting

Combine water and yeast in a large bowl. Let stand 5 minutes.

Stir in milk and butter. Stir in 2 cups flour, ½ cup sugar, eggs, and salt using a wooden spoon; stir for 2 minutes. Gradually stir in enough remaining flour to make a soft dough.

Turn dough out onto a lightly floured surface, and knead until smooth and elastic (about 8 minutes). Place in a well-greased bowl, turning to grease top.

Cover and let rise in a warm place (85 degrees), free from drafts, 45 minutes or until doubled in bulk.

Beat cream cheese, ¼ cup sugar, and egg yolk at medium speed with mixer until fluffy.

Punch dough down; turn out onto a lightly floured surface, and knead lightly 4 or 5 times. Divide dough into 4 equal portions. Roll 1 portion of dough into a 16- x 6-inch rectangle. Spread one-fourth of cream cheese mixture over dough, leaving a 1-inch border. Roll up dough, starting at short side, pressing firmly to eliminate air pockets; pinch ends to seal. Place dough, seam side down, on a lightly greased baking sheet. Repeat procedure with remaining dough.

Cut slits in top of each loaf at 1-inch intervals. Cover and let rise in a warm place, free from drafts, 30 minutes or until doubled in bulk.

Preheat oven to 350 degrees.

Bake for 16 to 18 minutes or until lightly browned. Cool completely on wire racks. Spread tops of loaves with chocolate frosting.
Yield: 4 loaves.

Wooden Gift Tags
Make these tasteful tags by painting wooden shapes with chalkboard paint. Once the paint dries, write a holiday message using chalk. Another option is to write a merry greeting on store-bought chalkboard tags.

THE SEASON IS THE REASON

*B*utterscotch morsels, nutmeg, cinnamon, and pumpkin reflect the flavors of the season, so keep autumn colors in mind when you buy the plate for presenting this cake. An ornament makes a great gift tag.

BUTTERSCOTCH-PUMPKIN CAKE

1	cup butterscotch morsels
2	cups all-purpose flour
1¾	cups granulated sugar
1	tablespoon baking powder
1	teaspoon salt
1½	teaspoons ground cinnamon
½	teaspoon ground nutmeg
1	cup canned mashed pumpkin
½	cup vegetable oil
3	large eggs
1	teaspoon vanilla extract

Powdered sugar

Preheat oven to 350 degrees. Microwave morsels in a small glass bowl on HIGH 30 to 60 seconds or until melted, stirring once. Cool.

Combine flour and next 5 ingredients in a bowl. Stir together melted morsels, pumpkin, and next 3 ingredients in a large bowl. Stir in flour mixture. Pour into a greased 12-cup Bundt pan.

Bake for 35 minutes or until a wooden pick inserted in center comes out clean. Cool in pan on a wire rack 15 minutes; remove from pan, and cool completely. Sprinkle with powdered sugar.
Yield: 1 (10-inch) cake.

SCRUMPTIOUS SHORTBREAD

These delicious bar cookies received our highest Test Kitchens rating for their indulgently buttery flair. Arrange these colorful treats on a cheery platter and deliver them to a friend.

RASPBERRY SHORTBREAD

- 1   cup butter, softened
- ⅔   cup granulated sugar
- 2½   cups all-purpose flour
- 1   (10-ounce) jar seedless raspberry jam, divided*
- 1½   cups powdered sugar
- 3½   tablespoons water
- ½   teaspoon almond extract

Preheat oven to 350 degrees.

Beat butter and granulated sugar at medium speed with an electric mixer until light and fluffy. Gradually add flour, beating at low speed until blended. Divide dough into 6 equal portions; roll each portion into a 12- x 1-inch strip. Place strips on lightly greased baking sheets.

Make a ½-inch-wide by ¼-inch-deep indentation down center of each strip using the handle of a wooden spoon. Spoon half of jam evenly into indentations.

Bake for 15 minutes. Remove from oven; spoon remaining jam into indentations. Bake 5 more minutes or until lightly browned.

Whisk together powdered sugar, water, and extract; drizzle over warm shortbread. Cut each strip

diagonally into 1-inch slices. Cool in pans on wire racks.
Yield: 6 dozen.

*Substitute any flavor jam or 1 (11¼-ounce) jar lemon curd for raspberry jam, if desired.

Apricot-Almond Shortbread: Gently coat unbaked shortbread strips with ¾ cup finely chopped almonds, pressing gently into shortbread. Make and fill indentations, substituting apricot jam for raspberry jam. Bake as directed.

SENSATIONAL SNACKING

Friends and neighbors will love to dig into this merry mix of dried berries, chocolate, and nuts! It's high in fiber, vitamins, and protein, and is perfect for an afternoon snack. And best of all, no baking is required! Seal the gorp in zip-top bags and place them in little gift sacks for multiple gifts.

GRAB 'N' GO GORP

2   cups crispy wheat cereal
    squares
2   cups mixed nuts
1   cup dried cherries
1   cup dried cranberries
1   cup dried blueberries
1   cup semisweet chocolate
    morsels

Combine all ingredients; store in an airtight container.
Yield: 8 cups.

WINTER WHITE

White chocolate, toasted macadamias, and orange essence bump this fudge up to fabulous. Line a white box with decorative tissue and place the fudge inside on a plate. Tie a bow around the box and match a gift tag to the tissue for a pretty presentation.

WHITE CHOCOLATE-MACADAMIA FUDGE

3	cups white chocolate morsels
1½	cups miniature marshmallows
1	(14-ounce) can sweetened condensed milk
2	teaspoons grated orange rind
1	teaspoon vanilla extract
⅛	teaspoon salt
1	cup chopped macadamia nuts, toasted

Line a 9-inch square pan with aluminum foil; lightly grease foil.

Cook first 3 ingredients in a heavy saucepan over medium heat, stirring constantly 10 to 11 minutes or until smooth. Remove from heat, and stir in orange rind, vanilla, and salt until blended. Stir in nuts.

Pour fudge into prepared pan. Cover and chill at least 4 hours or until firm. Cut fudge into squares, and store in refrigerator.
Yield: 2 pounds.

BANANA-NUT NIBBLES

Cakelike bars topped with cream cheese frosting and chopped pecans are perfect for the banana fan on your list. For fun and easy packaging, cut two slits into a purchased cardboard box lid, thread grosgrain ribbon through the slits, attach a cheerful card, and tie ribbon into a bow.

FROSTED BANANA BARS

½	cup butter or margarine, softened
2	cups sugar
3	large eggs
1½	cups mashed ripe banana
1	teaspoon vanilla extract
2	cups all-purpose flour
1	teaspoon baking soda
¼	teaspoon salt
	Vanilla Frosting
½	cup chopped pecans, toasted

Preheat oven to 350 degrees.

Beat butter at medium speed with an electric mixer until creamy; gradually add sugar, beating well. Add eggs, 1 at a time, beating until blended after each addition. Add banana and vanilla; beat well.

Combine flour, baking soda, and salt; gradually add to butter mixture, beating well.

Spread batter evenly into a lightly greased 15- x 10-inch jellyroll pan.

Bake for 22 to 25 minutes or until a wooden pick inserted in center comes out clean. Cool completely in pan on a wire rack. Spread Vanilla Frosting evenly over top. Sprinkle with pecans. Cut into bars. Store in refrigerator. *Yield:* 3 dozen.

Vanilla Frosting

1	(8-ounce) package cream cheese, softened
½	cup butter or margarine, softened
4	cups sifted powdered sugar
2	teaspoons vanilla extract

Beat cream cheese and butter at high speed with an electric mixer until soft and creamy. Gradually add powdered sugar, beating at low speed until light and fluffy. Stir in vanilla. *Yield:* 3 cups.

Frosted
Banana
Bars

SPRINKLED WITH RED AND GREEN

This savory bread is a cross between cornbread and focaccia. The basil and dried tomatoes bring out the colors of Christmas. Wrap it in tissue and deliver it on a festive tray.

PROVOLONE AND DRIED TOMATO-BASIL BREAD

⅓   cup dried tomatoes in oil,
       undrained
2¼   cups unbleached
       all-purpose flour
2   teaspoons baking powder
1   teaspoon salt
1   teaspoon pepper
½   teaspoon baking soda
1   cup (4 ounces) shredded
       provolone cheese
¼   cup chopped fresh parsley
1¼   teaspoons chopped fresh
       basil
2   large eggs
1¼   cups buttermilk
3   tablespoons vegetable oil
1   teaspoon sugar

Preheat oven to 350 degrees.
  Drain tomatoes, reserving 2 tablespoons oil; chop tomatoes, and set aside.
  Combine flour, baking powder, salt, pepper, and soda in a large bowl. Add chopped tomatoes, cheese, parsley, and basil.
  Whisk together reserved oil, eggs, buttermilk, vegetable oil, and sugar until smooth; add to dry ingredients, stirring just until moistened.
  Spread batter in a greased 8-inch round cakepan; smooth top of batter. Bake for 47 to 50 minutes or until light golden brown. Cool in pan on a wire rack 5 minutes.

Remove bread from pan; cool on wire rack.
Yield: 8 to 10 servings.

COLORFUL CHRISTMAS SPREAD

On the gift tag for this condiment, recommend it as a spread for rosemary focaccia or as a sauce for pork tenderloin.

RED ONION MARMALADE

2	tablespoons olive oil
8	cups thinly sliced red onion (about 2 pounds)
1	teaspoon fresh thyme leaves
1	bay leaf
¾	teaspoon fine sea salt
3	garlic cloves, minced
1	cup Cabernet Sauvignon or other dry red wine
¼	cup packed brown sugar
2	tablespoons balsamic vinegar
¼	teaspoon freshly ground pepper

Heat oil in a large nonstick skillet over medium heat. Add onion, thyme, and bay leaf. Cover and cook 25 minutes, stirring occasionally.

Stir in salt and garlic; cook, uncovered, 2 minutes, stirring frequently. Stir in wine, brown sugar, and vinegar; bring to a boil. Reduce heat; simmer 12 minutes or until liquid almost evaporates and becomes syrupy.

Remove from heat; stir in pepper. Cool to room temperature. Discard bay leaf. Store in refrigerator up to 1 week.
Yield: 3 cups.

BREAKFAST BAG

Laden with grated carrot, raisins, apples, and nuts, this slightly sweet batter bakes into 4 dozen charming muffins—enough for several friends.

COUNTRY MORNING MUFFINS

4	cups all-purpose flour
2½	cups sugar
4	teaspoons baking soda
4	teaspoons ground cinnamon
1	teaspoon salt
4	cups grated carrot (about 8 carrots)
1	cup raisins
1	cup chopped pecans
½	cup sweetened flaked coconut
2	Granny Smith apples, peeled and grated
6	large eggs
1¼	cups vegetable oil
2	teaspoons vanilla extract

Preheat oven to 375 degrees.

Combine first 5 ingredients in a large bowl; stir in carrot and next 4 ingredients and stir well. Combine eggs, oil, and vanilla; stir well. Add to flour mixture, stirring just until moistened.

Spoon batter into greased muffin pans, filling two-thirds full.

Bake for 20 to 25 minutes or until golden.

Yield: 4 dozen.

Christmas Towel Bag

It's easy to turn a Christmas hand towel into a little gift sack. Fold the towel in half and either stitch or use fabric glue to create the sack. Insert the item and seal with a matching ribbon.

BELLE OF THE BALL

*W*hat a bargain! From a basic cheese ball recipe, you can make three different balls by rolling one in cracked black pepper, one in chopped parsley, and the other in nuts. Variety is truly the spice of life! Deliver all three with an assortment of crackers.

THREE-IN-ONE CHEESE BALL

1   (8-ounce) package cream
      cheese, softened
4   cups (16 ounces) shredded
      Cheddar cheese, softened
2   tablespoons milk
2   tablespoons finely chopped
      onion
2   tablespoons Worcestershire
      sauce
2   teaspoons cracked pepper
      or coarsely ground pepper
½   cup crumbled blue cheese
2   tablespoons chopped fresh
      parsley
¼   teaspoon garlic powder
½   cup finely chopped
      pecans

Combine first 5 ingredients in a large mixing bowl; beat at medium speed with an electric mixer until creamy. Divide mixture evenly into thirds (about 1 cup each).

Shape 1 portion into a ball; roll in cracked pepper. Cover and chill 8 hours or until firm.

Add blue cheese to second portion, mixing well. Shape mixture into a ball, and roll in chopped parsley. Cover and chill 8 hours or until firm.

Add garlic powder to remaining portion, mixing well. Shape into a ball; roll in chopped pecans. Cover and chill 8 hours or until firm.

Remove from refrigerator 15 minutes before serving. Serve with crackers.
Yield: 3 cheese balls.

BOX OF BUNS

These rolls are delicious by themselves, but add a slice of roast beef and a dollop of horseradish, and you've got something special. Deliver them in a box wrapped with colorful Christmas paper.

ONION BUNS

2	(¼-ounce) envelopes active dry yeast
½	cup warm water (100 to 110 degrees)
1	teaspoon sugar
1	cup warm milk (100 to 110 degrees)
½	cup butter or margarine, melted
3	large eggs
½	cup sugar
1	teaspoon salt
5½	cups all-purpose flour
1	(1.4-ounce) envelope dry onion soup mix
¼	cup butter or margarine

Combine yeast, warm water, and 1 teaspoon sugar in a 1-cup glass measuring cup; let stand 5 minutes. Combine milk and ½ cup butter in a small bowl; stir well.

Combine yeast mixture, milk mixture, eggs, ½ cup sugar, salt, and 2 cups flour in a large mixing bowl; beat at medium speed with an electric mixer until well blended. Gradually stir in enough of remaining flour and onion soup mix to make a soft dough. Place in a well-greased bowl, turning to grease top. Cover and let rise in a warm place (85 degrees), free from drafts, 1 hour or until dough is doubled in bulk.

Punch dough down; turn out onto a heavily floured surface. Roll dough to ¾-inch thickness. Cut dough with a 2½-inch round cutter. Place rolls on greased baking sheets. Cover and let rise in a warm place, free from drafts, 30 minutes or until doubled in bulk.

Preheat oven to 350 degrees.

Bake for 14 minutes or until lightly browned. Rub butter across tops of buns while still hot. Serve buns warm.

Yield: 2½ dozen.

BREAD IN A BASKET

When you're eager to bake something special, this recipe will satisfy. Definitely a hands-on food, these crescents require kneading, rolling, punching, and folding to achieve ultimate tenderness. Most of the ingredients are probably in your kitchen already.

SOFT CRESCENTS

1   (¼-ounce) envelope active dry yeast
¼   cup warm water (100 to 110 degrees)
5   tablespoons sugar
1   teaspoon salt
¼   cup shortening
¾   cup milk
3¼ to 3¾ cups all-purpose flour
2   large eggs, lightly beaten
½   cup butter or margarine, melted
1   large egg, lightly beaten

Combine yeast and warm water in a 1-cup glass measuring cup; let stand 5 minutes.

Combine sugar, salt, shortening, and milk in a medium saucepan; cook over medium-low heat just until smooth, stirring constantly. Remove from heat.

Combine yeast mixture, sugar mixture, 2 cups flour, and 2 eggs in a large bowl; stir well. Gradually stir in enough of remaining flour to make a soft dough.

Turn dough out onto a lightly floured surface, and knead until smooth and elastic (about 4 minutes). Place in a well-greased bowl, turning to grease top. Cover and let rise in a warm place (85 degrees), free from drafts, 1 hour or until doubled in bulk.

Meanwhile, combine butter and 1 egg in a small bowl; stir well. Set aside.

Punch dough down. Divide dough into 3 equal portions. Roll each portion into a 10-inch circle. Brush each circle with butter mixture, reserving any remaining mixture; cut each into 8 wedges. Roll up each wedge tightly, beginning at wide end, and seal points. Place rolls, point side down, on lightly greased baking sheets, curving into crescent shapes.

Cover and let rise in a warm place, free from drafts, 30 minutes or until doubled in bulk. Brush rolls with remaining butter mixture.

Preheat oven to 400 degrees.

Bake for 8 minutes or until crescents are lightly browned. Cool slightly on baking sheets, and remove to wire racks to cool.
Yield: 2 dozen.

116

JOLLY GREEN JAR

Canned green chiles are usually a mild pepper, but when combined with three types of fragrant, aromatic seeds and some spices, they give this chutney a little kick.

GREEN CHILE CHUTNEY

¼	cup olive oil
4	large onions, coarsely chopped (about 7 cups)
3	garlic cloves, minced
4	(4.5-ounce) cans chopped green chiles, undrained
1	tablespoon mustard seeds
1	tablespoon coriander seeds
1	tablespoon fennel seeds
1	teaspoon ground cumin
1	teaspoon ground cinnamon
1	cup white vinegar
1	cup sugar
1	tablespoon salt

Heat olive oil in a small Dutch oven over medium heat, and sauté onion and garlic 15 minutes or until soft. Increase heat to medium-high. Add green chiles and next 5 ingredients; cook 5 minutes, stirring often. Stir in vinegar, sugar, and salt. Bring to a boil; cook 15 minutes, stirring occasionally. Pour into a sterilized container. Cool; store in refrigerator. Serve with roasted meats and poultry.
Yield: 3¾ cups.

Jar Toppers
It's easy to turn plain jars into clever Christmas wraps. Just cover the top with a small piece of decorative paper, and tie it on with a length of fringe or ribbon.

MERRY MINT

Here's an easy way to bake cheesecake for a whole host of gifts. Friends will love the chocolate cookie crust.

MINT CHEESECAKE BITES

3   cups cream-filled chocolate sandwich cookie crumbs (40 cookies)
½   cup butter or margarine, melted
4   (8-ounce) packages cream cheese, softened
1   cup sugar
4   large eggs
1½   teaspoons peppermint extract
6   drops green liquid food coloring
½   cup semisweet chocolate morsels
1   teaspoon shortening

Preheat oven to 350 degrees.

Stir together cookie crumbs and butter; press mixture into bottom of an aluminum foil-lined 13- x 9-inch pan.

Bake for 10 minutes. Cool on a wire rack. Reduce oven temperature to 300 degrees.

Beat cream cheese and sugar at medium speed with an electric mixer until creamy.

Add eggs, 1 at a time, beating just until blended after each addition.

Stir in peppermint extract and food coloring. Spread cream cheese mixture evenly over prepared crust.

Bake for 35 minutes or until set. Cool on a wire rack. Cover; chill 8 hours. Cut into squares.

Place chocolate morsels and shortening in a small zip-top freezer bag; seal. Submerge bag in hot water until chocolate melts; gently knead until mixture is smooth.

Snip a tiny hole in 1 corner of plastic bag; drizzle chocolate over cheesecake squares in a crisscross pattern, if desired. Store in refrigerator.

Yield: 24 servings.

Snowy Saucer

Paint a terra-cotta saucer using silver spray paint. Let dry. Wrap a length of silver ribbon around the edge of the saucer. Line the saucer with plastic wrap before adding food. Tie on a snowflake gift tag and a pair of silver beads.

PEACHY TREAT

This golden marmalade offers the essence of summer peaches year-round. You'll need 4½ cups of the cooked fruit mixture to jell correctly with the pectin. If you have a little fruit mixture left over, sweeten it and spoon it over pancakes or ice cream.

PEACH MARMALADE

1	orange
2	lemons
1	cup water
2	pounds fresh ripe peaches, peeled (6 medium)
7	cups sugar
1	(3-ounce) package liquid pectin

Cut orange and lemons into quarters; remove seeds and center pith. Process orange and lemon quarters in a food processor until ground; transfer to a Dutch oven. Add water, and bring to a boil. Cover, reduce heat, and simmer 20 minutes.

Cut peaches into quarters, removing pits; add peaches to food processor, and pulse 10 times or until chopped. Add peaches to citrus mixture. Measure 4½ cups of fruit mixture to use for marmalade. Reserve any leftover fruit mixture for other uses. Stir sugar into 4½ cups fruit mixture; bring to a rolling boil.

Add liquid pectin to peach mixture; return to a boil, and boil 1 minute, stirring constantly. Remove from heat, and skim off foam with a metal spoon.

Pour hot marmalade into hot sterilized jars, filling to ¼ inch from top; wipe jar rims. Cover jars at once with metal lids, and screw on bands. Process the jars in boiling water bath for 5 minutes. *Yield:* 9 half-pints.

Fabric Toppers
Cut small squares of fabrics, and place them over the jars. Tie with ribbon and a little gift tag.

120

RELISH THE SEASON

This low-fat dish is a great make-ahead gift. Once the relish has cooled, simply scoop it into an airtight container, and add a label and a ribbon.

NEW-FASHIONED CORN RELISH

1	small onion, chopped (about 1 cup)
½	cup sugar
½	cup apple cider vinegar
2	teaspoons celery seeds
½	teaspoon mustard seeds
1	(15.25-ounce) can whole kernel corn, drained

½	cup chopped celery
¼	cup sweet pickle relish
1	(2-ounce) jar diced pimiento, drained

Stir together first 5 ingredients in a medium saucepan; bring to a boil. Reduce heat, and simmer, uncovered, 10 minutes.

Stir together corn and remaining 3 ingredients in a large bowl; pour hot vinegar mixture over corn mixture, and stir gently. Let cool completely (about 2 hours). Store in an airtight container in refrigerator.
Yield: 2½ cups.

CITRUS COOKIES

Get a head start on your holiday baking, as you can freeze these logs of dough up to two months. After you bake them, wrap the cookies in a little gift box, and tie on a lemon embellishment.

LEMON ICEBOX COOKIES

1	cup butter, softened
1	cup granulated sugar
1	cup firmly packed light brown sugar
2	large eggs
1	teaspoon grated lemon rind
2	tablespoons fresh lemon juice
3½	cups all-purpose flour
1	teaspoon baking soda
½	teaspoon salt

Beat butter and sugars at medium speed with an electric mixer until fluffy. Add eggs, 1 at a time, beating well after each addition. Add lemon rind and lemon juice, beating until blended.

Combine flour, baking soda, and salt; gradually add to butter mixture, beating just until blended.

Divide dough into 3 equal portions; roll each into a 10-inch log on wax paper. Cover; chill 8 hours. Cut each log into ½-inch slices; place on greased baking sheets.

Preheat oven to 350 degrees.

Bake for 11 to 12 minutes or until edges are lightly browned. Remove to wire racks to cool. Store in an airtight container. *Yield:* 5 dozen.

TAKE A STAND

If mayonnaise seems like an odd ingredient, don't be alarmed; it adds flavor and moisture to this cranberry-orange cake. Deliver on a decoupaged cake stand.

CRANBERRY SAUCE CAKE

3	cups all-purpose flour
1½	cups granulated sugar
1	cup mayonnaise
1	(16-ounce) can whole-berry cranberry sauce
1	tablespoon grated orange rind
⅓	cup orange juice
1	teaspoon baking soda
1	teaspoon salt
1	teaspoon orange extract
1	cup chopped walnuts
1	cup sifted powdered sugar
2	tablespoons orange juice

Preheat oven to 350 degrees. Grease and flour a Bundt pan. Combine flour and next 8 ingredients in a large bowl. Beat at medium speed with an electric mixer until well blended. Fold in walnuts. Spoon batter into prepared Bundt pan.

Bake 55 to 57 minutes or until a wooden pick inserted in center comes out clean. Cool cake in pan on a wire rack 10 minutes; remove cake from pan. Cool cake completely on wire rack.

Combine powdered sugar and orange juice; stir well. Spoon glaze over cooled cake, allowing it to drizzle down sides of cake. *Yield:* 1 (10-inch) cake.

Decoupaged Cake Stand

Following manufacturer's instructions, decoupage Christmas wrapping paper or other design around the underside of a cake stand. (Be sure to decorate only the underside because decoupage materials aren't food safe.)

BUNDLED IN A BOWL

These croutons, coated with cinnamon and sugar, add a delightful crispiness to both sweet and savory soups as well as tangy-sweet salads. We've included a recipe for Pumpkin Soup that's divine with the crispy nuggets. Package them in a plastic sack, place them inside a soup bowl, and include the Pumpkin Soup recipe as part of the gift.

SWEET CROUTONS

4   cups French bread cubes
3   tablespoons butter or
     margarine, melted
¼   cup sugar
½   teaspoon ground cinnamon

Preheat oven to 375 degrees. Toss together bread cubes and melted butter. Combine sugar and cinnamon; add to bread cubes, tossing to coat. Spread in a single layer on a lightly greased baking sheet.

Bake, stirring occasionally, for 15 minutes or until golden brown. *Yield:* 3 cups.

Pumpkin Soup Stock

2   celery ribs
2   carrots
1   large onion
1   medium parsnip
1   large leek
2   garlic cloves
5   cups water
½   cup chopped fresh parsley
2   tablespoons grated fresh
     ginger
2   tablespoons lemon or lime
     juice
1   teaspoon salt
3   or 4 chicken wings
2   cups canned pumpkin

Chop first 5 ingredients; mince garlic.

Bring chopped vegetables, minced garlic, 5 cups water, and next 5 ingredients to a boil in a large Dutch oven over medium heat; cover mixture, reduce heat, and simmer 2 hours. Discard chicken wings. Stir in pumpkin.

Process mixture, in small batches, in a blender or food processor until smooth, stopping to scrape down sides. Cool. Chill up to 5 days or freeze up to 3 months. *Yield:* 10 cups.

Pumpkin Soup with Sweet Croutons

4   cups Pumpkin Soup Stock
1   cup milk
1   tablespoon grated fresh
     ginger (we tested with
     Spice World)
½   teaspoon salt
½   teaspoon sugar
½   teaspoon curry powder
¼   teaspoon ground black
     pepper
¼   teaspoon ground
     cinnamon
⅛   teaspoon ground red
     pepper
Sweet croutons

Cook first 9 ingredients in a large saucepan over medium heat 20 minutes or until thoroughly heated. Serve with Sweet Croutons. *Yield:* 5 cups.

Pumpkin Soup
with Sweet Croutons

4 cups pumpkin soup stock
1 cup milk
1 tablespoon fresh ginger
1/2 teaspoon salt
1/2 teaspoon sugar

MUG OF MOCHA

*H*ere's a homemade instant coffee blend that's not as strong on coffee flavor, so you'll taste the cocoa and vanilla with each sip. Paint a colorful mug with a Christmas design, and add a bag of this delicious blend for the coffee connoisseurs on your list.

MOCHA COFFEE BLEND

1	cup powdered non-dairy coffee creamer
¾	cup sugar
½	cup instant coffee granules
3	tablespoons cocoa
1	vanilla bean

Process first 4 ingredients in an electric blender until blended. Split vanilla bean lengthwise, and cut into 3 pieces. Stir vanilla bean pieces into coffee mixture. Transfer coffee blend to a jar; cover and let stand at least 24 hours before using. *Yield:* 2 cups.

Directions for recipe card: To serve, spoon 3 tablespoons coffee blend into a cup. Add ¾ cup boiling water; stir well.

COFFEE BITES

There's a little espresso bean crunch in the center of each chocolate nugget. Recipients will get a burst of coffee flavor in each delectable bite.

ESPRESSO CRUNCH CUPS

¼   cup butter or margarine, softened
2¼   cups sifted powdered sugar
3   tablespoons Kahlúa
¾   cup crushed chocolate-covered espresso beans (4 ounces)
⅛   teaspoon salt
2   cups semisweet chocolate morsels
6   ounces chocolate bark coating, chopped
48   (1½") paper candy cups

Beat butter at medium speed with an electric mixer about 2 minutes or until creamy. Gradually add powdered sugar alternately with Kahlúa, beating until smooth. Stir in espresso beans and salt. Cover and chill 1 hour or until firm. Shape mixture by teaspoonfuls into balls, and flatten slightly.

Melt chocolate morsels and chocolate coating in a small saucepan over low heat, stirring just until smooth. Spoon ½ teaspoon melted chocolate into 48 paper-lined miniature (1¾") muffin pans; gently tap pans on counter to smooth out chocolate.

Place 1 Kahlúa ball in each cup; spoon remaining melted chocolate over Kahlúa balls, covering them completely. Cover and chill chocolate cups until firm. Store in an airtight container in refrigerator. *Yield:* 4 dozen.

Scarf Wrap
Tie a disposable container with a sheer scarf. Use a coordinating sheer ribbon to tie the package together, and add a gift tag.

COOKIE COLLECTION

Cupfuls of 10 hearty ingredients combine to make these everything-but-the-kitchen-sink cookies. This recipe makes a lot, so package several batches in gift sacks.

10-CUP COOKIES

1   cup granulated sugar
1   cup firmly packed light
      brown sugar
1   cup shortening
1   cup peanut butter
3   large eggs, lightly beaten
1   cup all-purpose flour
1   cup uncooked quick-
      cooking oats
2   teaspoons baking soda
1   teaspoon baking powder
1   cup chopped pecans
1   cup sweetened flaked
      coconut
1   cup raisins
1   cup semisweet chocolate
      morsels

Preheat oven to 350 degrees.

Combine first 4 ingredients in a large mixing bowl; beat at medium speed with an electric mixer until creamy. Add eggs, beating well.

Combine flour and next 3 ingredients; add to peanut butter mixture, and beat well. Stir in pecans and remaining ingredients.

Drop dough by level tablespoonfuls onto lightly greased baking sheets. Bake for 10 to 12 minutes or until golden. Immediately remove to wire racks to cool. *Yield:* 5½ dozen.

See-Thru Sack

Cut a square out of the center of a gift sack. Cut a frame out of the center of a piece of decorative paper to match the hole in the sack. Glue the frame in place. Glue a piece of cellophane to the inside of the sack to cover the hole.

CHOCOLATE-CINNAMON SENSATION

These treats resemble turnovers that you can eat out of hand. Refrigerated cinnamon rolls are the speedy secret behind this quick-to-make gift. Deliver them in an old-fashioned tin.

CHOCOLATE-CINNAMON HAND PIES

1   (12-ounce) can refrigerated cinnamon rolls
½   cup semisweet chocolate morsels
½   cup chopped pecans (optional)

Preheat oven to 400 degrees.

Separate cinnamon rolls, reserving glaze packet. Roll each round of dough into a 3½-inch circle on a floured surface, cinnamon side up.

Spoon 1 tablespoon chocolate morsels in middle of each circle. Fold in 2 sides, and roll up. Place pies, seam side down, on a greased baking sheet. Roll in pecans, if desired.

Bake for 14 to 18 minutes or until golden. Drizzle reserved glaze over pies.

Yield: 8 servings.

COVERED WITH COCONUT

*S̲turdy pound cakes travel well and are always a welcome gift.
A glaze of lemon and coconut makes this version especially tasty.*

LEMON-COCONUT POUND CAKE

1½   cups butter or margarine, softened
1   (8-ounce) package cream cheese, softened
3   cups sugar
6   large eggs
3   cups all-purpose flour
¼   teaspoon salt
1   tablespoon lemon juice
1   tablespoon vanilla extract
½   teaspoon coconut extract
¾   cup sweetened flaked coconut

Glaze
½   cup sweetened flaked coconut

Preheat oven to 325 degrees.

Beat butter and cream cheese at medium speed with an electric mixer 2 minutes or until creamy. Gradually add sugar, beating 3 to 5 minutes. Add eggs, 1 at a time, beating just until yellow disappears.

Combine flour and salt. Gradually add to butter mixture, mixing at low speed just until blended. Stir in lemon juice, extracts, and ¾ cup coconut.

Pour batter into a greased and floured 10-inch tube pan. Bake for 1 hour and 20 to 25 minutes or until a long wooden pick inserted in center comes out clean. Cool in pan on a wire rack 10 minutes; remove from pan, and cool completely on wire rack.

Spoon Glaze over top of cake, allowing it to drizzle down sides. Sprinkle top of cake with ½ cup flaked coconut.
Yield: 1 (10-inch) cake.

Glaze
1   cup sifted powdered sugar
1   tablespoon butter or margarine, melted
2   teaspoons grated lemon rind
2   tablespoons lemon juice
1   teaspoon coconut extract

Combine all ingredients in a small bowl; stir until smooth.
Yield: ⅓ cup.

Fit to Be Tied
Cut several slits, equal distances apart, and large enough for the desired length of ribbon, around the center of a cake box top. Run a ribbon through the slits. Tie a bow in the center, and embellish with Christmas ornaments.

SPICE UP THE HOLIDAYS

*T*wo types of pepper and a bit of hot sauce add lots of zip to this dip. Pour it into a small clamp-top container, and package it with breadsticks bundled in a burlap bag.

SPICY DIPPING SAUCE

1	cup mayonnaise
1	green onion, thinly sliced
1	tablespoon white wine vinegar
2	teaspoons Dijon mustard
½	teaspoon ground red pepper
¼	teaspoon freshly ground black pepper
½	teaspoon hot pepper sauce (we tested with Crystal)

Combine all ingredients in a bowl; cover and chill at least 1 hour. Store in refrigerator.
Yield: 1¼ cups.

TAKE OUT A SWEET TREAT

The fresh orange flavor of these sugared walnuts signal the holiday season. It's easiest to grate the orange for the rind before juicing. Package these candies in decorative carryout containers.

ORANGE-SUGARED WALNUTS

3	cups sugar
½	cup water
½	cup fresh orange juice
1	pound walnut halves
1	teaspoon grated orange rind

Combine first 3 ingredients in a large heavy saucepan. Cook over low heat, stirring gently, until sugar dissolves. Cover and cook over medium heat 2 to 3 minutes to wash down sugar crystals from sides of pan.

Uncover and cook, stirring constantly, until a candy thermometer registers 238 degrees (soft ball stage). Remove pan from heat, and stir in walnut halves and orange rind with a wooden spoon just until mixture begins to thicken. Pour candy onto greased wax paper. Working rapidly, separate walnuts with 2 forks. Let candy stand until firm. *Yield:* 2 pounds.

GRAPEFRUIT GREETINGS

Fresh tarragon reigns supreme in this supereasy salad topper. Pour it into a glass cruet, and add a personalized label. For a decorative touch, wrap a small string of beads with a festive trinket around the neck of the cruet.

GRAPEFRUIT-RASPBERRY VINAIGRETTE

3	tablespoons grapefruit or orange juice
1	tablespoon raspberry vinegar
¼	cup olive oil
2	teaspoons chopped fresh tarragon
⅛	teaspoon salt
⅛	teaspoon freshly ground pepper

Combine grapefruit juice and vinegar in a small bowl. Gradually add oil, stirring with a wire whisk until blended. Stir in tarragon, salt, and pepper. Cover and chill up to 1 week.
Yield: ½ cup.

CHOCK-FULL OF CHIPS

Similar to a macaroon, these cranberry-studded delights are slightly crisp on the outside and soft in the middle. Make sure to store them in an airtight container to keep them fresh. Line a decorative container with tissue, and pile the cookies inside.

CRANBERRY CHIP COOKIES

½	cup butter or margarine, softened
½	cup sugar
1	large egg
1	teaspoon vanilla extract
1	cup all-purpose flour
1	cup uncooked quick-cooking oats
1	teaspoon baking powder
1	cup white chocolate morsels
½	cup dried cranberries
½	cup flaked coconut

Preheat oven to 350 degrees. Beat first 4 ingredients at medium speed with an electric mixer until creamy.

Combine flour, oats, and baking powder. Gradually add flour mixture to butter mixture, beating at low speed until soft dough forms. Stir in white chocolate morsels, cranberries, and coconut.

Drop dough by heaping teaspoonfuls 2 inches apart onto ungreased baking sheets. Bake for 9 to 11 minutes or until set. Cool on baking sheets 2 minutes; remove to wire racks to cool completely.
Yield: 3 dozen.

RING IN THE SEASON

*N*ow here's a great make-ahead gift. Simply wrap these chewy treats in plastic wrap, place them in a zip-top freezer bag, and freeze up to three months. Package them in a small decorative pan, and deliver to a friend for a sweet holiday treat.

WALNUT-DATE BARS

1   (18.25-ounce) package
     yellow cake mix
⅔   cup firmly packed brown
     sugar
2   large eggs
¾   cup butter or margarine,
     melted
2   cups chopped dates,
     divided
2   cups chopped walnuts or
     pecans, divided

Preheat oven to 350 degrees.
Combine cake mix and brown sugar in a mixing bowl. Add eggs and melted butter, beating at medium speed with an electric mixer until blended (batter will be stiff). Spoon half of batter into a lightly greased 13- x 9-inch pan; sprinkle with 1 cup each of dates and walnuts. Press mixture gently.

Stir remaining 1 cup each of dates and walnuts into remaining batter; spread over mixture in pan.

Bake for 35 to 38 minutes or until golden. Run a knife around edge of pan to loosen sides. Let stand 30 minutes before cutting. Cut into squares, and store in an airtight container.
Yield: 16 servings.

Jingle Bell Tag
Glue tiny jingle bells on a small piece of cardstock to create a clever little gift card. String several jingle bells onto a narrow length of ribbon, and use it to tie on the card.

SHAKE IT UP

*F*riends will enjoy sprinkling this flavorful seasoning on all types of meats, vegetables, and salads. Pour the salt into inexpensive shakers found at flea markets. Trim the tops with colorful beads and wire. Add a small label and some ribbon.

GOURMET SEASONING SALT

1	cup salt
2	teaspoons dry mustard
1½	teaspoons dried oregano
1	teaspoon dried marjoram
1	teaspoon dried thyme
1	teaspoon garlic powder
1	teaspoon curry powder
½	teaspoon onion powder
½	teaspoon celery seeds
¼	teaspoon dried dillweed

Combine all ingredients, stirring until well blended. Store in an airtight container.
Yield: 1¼ cups.

gourmet seasoning salt

BASKING IN BASIL

*J*ust two ingredients mingle
to make a dipping sauce that will
complement all kinds of bread.
Pour into a decorative bottle, tie
with ribbon, and deliver in a
basket adorned with fresh basil.

BASIL DIPPING OIL

4   cups chopped fresh basil
    leaves (about 2
    [¾-ounce] packages)
1   cup olive oil

Combine basil and oil in a small
heavy saucepan. Cook over
medium-low heat until thermometer
registers 180 degrees. Reduce heat
to low; cook 20 minutes (do not
allow temperature to rise above 200
degrees). Cool to room temperature.
Drain oil mixture through a sieve
into a bowl; discard solids. Store in
refrigerator.
Yield: 1 cup.

FRUIT CRISP KIT

Create a gift basket of berry filling and oatmeal-walnut topping to turn into a warm winter fruit crisp. All the recipient needs to do is add a bit of butter. Don't forget to include the recipe for Winter Fruit Crisp.

MIXED BERRY FILLING

½   cup sugar
¼   cup plus 2 tablespoons all-purpose flour
2   (12-ounce) containers cranberry-raspberry crushed fruit (we tested with Ocean Spray)
2   cups frozen blueberries

Combine sugar and flour in a medium bowl, stirring well. Add remaining ingredients, mixing well. Chill until ready to prepare crisp. *Yield:* 4 cups.

OATMEAL-WALNUT CRUMBLE TOPPING

1   cup uncooked regular oats
¼   cup firmly packed brown sugar
3   tablespoons all-purpose flour
¼   teaspoon ground cinnamon
Dash of salt
½   cup chopped walnuts

Combine all ingredients in a medium bowl, stirring well. *Yield:* 2 cups.

Winter Fruit Crisp

1   recipe Mixed Berry Filling
¼   cup butter
1   recipe Oatmeal-Walnut Crumble Topping

Preheat oven to 350 degrees. Spoon fruit filling into a lightly greased 9-inch square pan. Cut butter into Oatmeal-Walnut Crumble Topping using a pastry blender or 2 knives until mixture is crumbly. Sprinkle topping evenly over filling. Bake for 35 minutes or until golden and bubbly. Serve warm with vanilla ice cream. *Yield:* 6 servings.

SPICY STICKS

These are perfect companions for gumbo, stew, or chili. They're shaped like candy canes, but they're spicy-hot rather than sweet! Create a complete gift set by lining a tin container with a dishtowel and embellishing with some seasonal berries or flowers.

SPICY CANDY CANE BREADSTICKS

1   (11-ounce) can refrigerated breadstick dough
1   large egg, lightly beaten
2   tablespoons paprika
2   tablespoons seasoned pepper blend* (we tested with McCormick)

Preheat oven to 375 degrees.
Separate breadsticks; working with 2 at a time, roll each breadstick into a 20-inch rope. Brush ropes with egg. Twist ropes together, pinching ends to seal. Repeat with remaining breadsticks.
Combine paprika and pepper blend; spread mixture on a paper plate. Roll breadsticks in pepper mixture, pressing gently to coat. (Wash hands between rolling each breadstick, if necessary.)
Place breadsticks on a greased baking sheet, curving top of each breadstick to form a candy cane shape. Bake for 10 to 12 minutes or until golden.
Yield: 6 servings.
*If you can't find seasoned pepper blend, combine equal portions of cracked black pepper, sweet red pepper flakes, and salt.

SENSATIONAL SAUCES

These sauces—some sweet, some savory—are simple to prepare and sure to please. Deliver your homemade treats in a fun container complete with ribbons and pretty tags.

CARAMEL SAUCE

1 cup butter
2 cups sugar
2 teaspoons fresh lemon juice
1½ cups whipping cream

Melt butter in a heavy saucepan over medium heat; add sugar and lemon juice, and cook, stirring constantly, about 7 minutes or until mixture turns a light caramel color, or about 8½ minutes for a medium color, or up to about 10 minutes for a dark color. (The medium color produced the most popular flavor among our taste testers.) Gradually add cream, and cook, stirring constantly, 1 to 2 minutes or until smooth. Remove from heat, and cool. Pour sauce into sterilized jars, cover, and store in refrigerator up to 1 month.
Yield: about 3 cups.

Note: Be very careful when adding the whipping cream to the hot caramel sauce. It creates steam, and the liquid will splatter slightly.

CUMBERLAND SAUCE

2½ cups port wine, divided
1 (10½-ounce) jar red currant jelly
3 tablespoons light brown sugar
2 tablespoons grated orange rind
⅔ cup orange juice
1½ tablespoons grated fresh ginger
2 teaspoons dry mustard
¼ teaspoon salt
¼ teaspoon ground red pepper
2½ tablespoons cornstarch

Bring 2 cups wine and next 8 ingredients to a boil in a large saucepan, stirring constantly; reduce heat, and simmer, stirring often, 20 minutes.
Stir together remaining ½ cup wine and cornstarch until smooth. Stir into hot mixture; bring to a boil over medium heat. Boil, stirring constantly, 1 minute; cool. Pour sauce into sterilized jars, cover, and store in refrigerator up to 1 month.
Yield: about 4 cups.

APPLESAUCE

12 large Granny Smith apples, peeled and coarsely chopped
1½ cups sugar
¼ cup fresh lemon juice

Cook all ingredients in a Dutch oven over low heat, stirring often, 10 minutes. (Sugar will dissolve, and apples will begin to break down and release juices.) Increase to medium heat, and cook, stirring often, 25 more minutes or until thickened. Spoon into sterilized jars, cover, and store in refrigerator up to 1 month.
Yield: about 6 cups.

Safe Sauces
Don't overlook safety when giving homemade sauces as gifts. Sterilize jars by boiling them, covered with water, for 15 minutes. Fill jars while still hot. Cover and refrigerate sauces immediately, and be sure that your friends and relatives know to keep them cold. It's easy for a small gift to be lost in the holiday shuffle, so hand deliver yours, and ask that it be stored in the refrigerator right away.

CHRISTMAS CRUNCH

Sprinkle some of this "reindeer food" outdoors on Christmas Eve and children's faces will light up when they see just crumbs left in the morning. Trim little paper sacks with ribbon, beads, and rickrack. It makes enough for lots of little friends.

MAGIC REINDEER FOOD

2   (24-ounce) packages vanilla bark coating
3   cups mini pretzels
1   (12-ounce) can cocktail peanuts
1   (14.25-ounce) package frosted toasted oat O-shaped cereal
1   (15-ounce) package crisp rice cereal squares
1   (14-ounce) package holiday candy-coated chocolate pieces
Red and green sugars

Place vanilla coating in a glass container; microwave at HIGH 2½ minutes or until melted, stirring once.

Combine pretzels and next 3 ingredients in a large bowl; add melted vanilla coating, tossing to coat. Stir in chocolate pieces.

Spread mixture onto wax paper; sprinkle with sugars. Let stand 30 minutes. Break into pieces. *Yield:* 25 cups.

POPCORN PRESENTS

Package this crispy treat in cellophane bags tied with raffia for inexpensive gifts. Place them inside paint tins lined with colorful fabric.

CARAMEL POPCORN

3	quarts freshly popped popcorn
1	cup blanched slivered almonds
1	cup pecan halves
1	cup cashews
½	cup butter or margarine
1	cup firmly packed brown sugar
¼	cup honey
1	teaspoon vanilla extract

Preheat oven to 250 degrees.

Toss first 4 ingredients together in a lightly greased 14- x 11-inch roasting pan.

Melt butter in a medium saucepan over low heat. Stir in brown sugar and honey. Bring to a boil, and boil 5 minutes without stirring. Stir in vanilla. Pour syrup over popcorn mixture, stirring until evenly coated.

Bake for 1 hour, stirring every 15 minutes. Cool completely, and break into pieces. Store in airtight containers.

Yield: about 4 quarts.

JOLLY JAR OF SAUCE

This dipping sauce is true to its name—it's hard to resist double dipping. Pour it into a jar embellished with ribbon and a festive ornament. Pair it with a batch of purchased chicken fingers for a welcome holiday snack or meal.

COME BACK SAUCE

1	cup mayonnaise
½	cup olive oil
⅓	cup chili sauce
¼	cup ketchup
2	tablespoons water
4	teaspoons Worcestershire sauce
4	teaspoons prepared mustard
2	teaspoons coarsely ground pepper
⅛	teaspoon paprika
¼	teaspoon hot sauce
1	medium onion, minced
2	garlic cloves, minced

Stir together all ingredients. Cover and chill 1 hour or up to 4 days.
Yield: 3 cups.

146

SWEET "PIZZA PARTY"

This dessert pizza is studded with chopped candy bars and drizzled with caramel. It cuts easily into slices and is a favorite of kids and adults alike. Place it on a platter, and embellish it with a string of foam trinkets and colorful tissue. Tell the recipient to chill it until ready to serve.

CANDY BAR PIZZA

1	(18-ounce) package refrigerated chocolate chip cookie dough
2	cups frozen whipped topping, thawed
2	(2.7-ounce) chocolate-coated caramel-peanut nougat bars, chopped (we tested with Snickers bars)
2	(1.4-ounce) chocolate-covered toffee candy bars, chopped (we tested with Skor bars)
2	(2.1-ounce) chocolate-covered crispy peanut-buttery candy bars, chopped (we tested with Butterfinger bars)
¼	cup caramel topping

Preheat oven to 375 degrees. Press cookie dough onto a greased 12-inch pizza pan. Bake for 15 to 18 minutes. Let cool completely.

Spread whipped topping evenly over cookie dough. Sprinkle candies over topping. Drizzle lightly with caramel topping. Refrigerate pizza until ready to serve. To serve, cut into slices. *Yield:* 10 to 12 servings.

TRAY CHIC

Coconut and almonds give this moist cake the flavor of macaroon cookies. Cut it into squares, place them on a festive tray, and deliver to a coconut-loving friend.

DOUBLE MACAROON COFFEE CAKE

¾   cup butter or margarine, softened
1¼   cups sugar, divided
2   large eggs
2⅓   cups all-purpose flour, divided
2½   teaspoons baking powder
½   teaspoon baking soda
½   teaspoon salt, divided
1   cup sour cream
¼   teaspoon coconut extract
¾   teaspoon almond extract, divided
2   cups sweetened flaked coconut
⅔   cup sweetened condensed milk
½   cup slivered almonds, chopped
¼   cup butter or margarine, cut into pieces

Preheat oven to 350 degrees.
Beat ¾ cup butter at medium speed with an electric mixer until creamy. Gradually add 1 cup sugar, beating well. Add eggs, 1 at a time, beating until blended after each addition.

Combine 2 cups flour, baking powder, baking soda, and ¼ teaspoon salt; add to butter mixture alternately with sour cream, beginning and ending with flour mixture. Beat at low speed until blended after each addition. Stir in coconut extract and ½ teaspoon almond extract.
Spoon half of batter into a greased 9-inch square pan.
Combine flaked coconut, sweetened condensed milk, remaining ¼ teaspoon salt, and remaining ¼ teaspoon almond extract; stir well. Spread over batter in pan. Spread remaining batter over coconut mixture.
Combine chopped almonds, remaining ¼ cup sugar, and remaining ⅓ cup flour. Cut ¼ cup butter into flour mixture with a pastry blender until crumbly. Spread mixture over batter.
Bake for 45 minutes or until a wooden pick inserted in center comes out clean. Cool in pan on a wire rack. Cut into squares.
Yield: 9 servings.

CHRISTMAS CRANBERRIES

The surprise comes from the macaroon crust that forms on top and the addition of blueberries and coconut to the filling. Deliver in a pieplate tied with ribbon and an ornament.

CRANBERRY SURPRISE PIE

3	cups fresh or frozen coarsely chopped cranberries
½	cup fresh or frozen blueberries
½	cup chopped pecans or sliced almonds
⅓	cup flaked coconut
1½	cups sugar
1	large egg
½	cup all-purpose flour
6	tablespoons butter or margarine, melted

Preheat oven to 325 degrees. Combine cranberries and blueberries. Spoon cranberry mixture into a lightly greased 9-inch pieplate. Combine pecans and coconut, and sprinkle over cranberry mixture. Top with 1 cup sugar.

Beat egg and remaining ½ cup sugar at medium speed with an electric mixer until blended. Add flour and butter; beat at low speed until blended. Spread batter evenly over pie filling. Bake for 1 hour or until golden. Cool completely on a wire rack. Store in refrigerator. *Yield:* 8 servings.

CHRISTMAS COOKIES

Lemon adds a refreshing tang to this traditional sugar cookie recipe. A glass cookie jar makes a great container for these holiday goodies. Wrap the top with a string of narrow beads, and repeat the beads on the gift tag.

SUGAR COOKIES

- ⅔ cup butter, softened
- ¾ cup sugar
- 1 large egg
- 4 teaspoons milk
- ½ teaspoon vanilla extract
- ½ teaspoon lemon extract
- 2 cups all-purpose flour
- 1½ teaspoons baking powder
- ¼ teaspoon salt

Sugar

Beat butter and ¾ cup sugar at medium speed with an electric mixer until creamy. Add egg; beat well. Add milk, vanilla, and lemon extract; beat well.

Combine flour, baking powder, and salt; stir into butter mixture. Cover and chill 1 hour.

Preheat oven to 375 degrees.

Divide dough into 4 equal portions. Work with 1 portion at a time, storing remaining portions in refrigerator. Roll each portion to ⅛-inch thickness on a lightly floured surface. Cut with a 2½-inch cookie cutter; place on ungreased baking sheets. Sprinkle with sugar.

Bake for 10 minutes or until edges are lightly browned. Cool 1 minute; remove cookies to wire racks to cool completely.
Yield: 2 dozen.

NEW YEAR'S SURPRISE

The flavors of chilies and lime add Southwestern zest to this sensational salsa. Pack the salsa in a jar, and deliver with a bag of homemade pita chips for lots of luck in the new year.

BLACK-EYED PEA-AVOCADO SALSA

2	(15.5-ounce) cans black-eyed peas with jalapeño peppers, rinsed and drained
1	(10-ounce) can diced tomatoes and green chilies
2	avocados, diced
1	small green bell pepper, diced
½	small red onion, diced
¾	cup zesty Italian salad dressing
1	tablespoon fresh lime juice

Stir together all ingredients. Cover and chill until ready to serve or up to 2 days.
Yield: 6 cups.

EASY BAKED PITA CHIPS

4	(7-inch) whole wheat or white pita rounds
½	cup grated Parmesan cheese

Preheat oven to 350 degrees. Separate each pita into 2 rounds. Cut each round into 8 wedges to make 64 triangles. Arrange in a single layer on ungreased baking sheets. Coat with cooking spray; sprinkle evenly with ½ cup grated cheese. Bake for 12 minutes. Let cool before storing in an airtight container.
Yield: 64 chips.

CAMPFIRE COOKIES

Enjoy this cookie version of the favorite campfire treat in the comfort of your own home. Our version has a chunky peanut butter crust that's layered with marshmallow cream, chocolate, and peanuts. Wrap them in a box, and tie on a decorative gift tag.

S'MORES COOKIES

½	cup butter or margarine, softened
½	cup granulated sugar
½	cup firmly packed brown sugar
½	cup chunky peanut butter
1	large egg
½	teaspoon vanilla extract
1½	cups all-purpose flour
2	teaspoons baking powder
½	teaspoon salt
1	(7-ounce) jar marshmallow cream
1	cup semisweet chocolate morsels
¾	cup salted roasted peanuts

Preheat oven to 375 degrees. Beat butter at medium speed with an electric mixer until creamy; add sugars, beating well. Add peanut butter, egg, and vanilla; beat mixture well.

Combine flour, baking powder, and salt; add to butter mixture, beating well.

Press dough into a greased 13- x 9-inch pan. Spread marshmallow cream over dough. Sprinkle chocolate morsels and peanuts over marshmallow cream. Bake for 16 to 18 minutes or until marshmallow cream is lightly browned. Cool completely in pan on a wire rack; cut into bars. *Yield:* 2 dozen.

CHOCOLATE SENSATION

Chocolate cake mix and pudding mix add to the convenient nature of this rich, moist Bundt cake. The final chocolate in the trio? Two full cups of morsels that melt throughout the cake as it bakes. Deliver this rich dessert on a ribbon-lined cake plate for a perfect presentation.

TRIPLE CHOCOLATE CAKE

1   (18.25-ounce) package chocolate cake mix (we tested with Duncan Hines)
1   (3.9-ounce) package chocolate instant pudding mix
1   (8-ounce) container sour cream
4   large eggs
½   cup water
½   cup vegetable oil
2   cups semisweet chocolate morsels
½   cup chopped pecans
Cocoa
Chocolate Glaze

Preheat oven to 350 degrees.

Combine first 6 ingredients in a large bowl; beat for 1 minute until ingredients are blended. Stir in chocolate morsels and pecans. Spoon batter into a well-greased 12-cup Bundt pan dusted lightly with cocoa.

Bake for 1 hour or until cake begins to pull away from sides of pan. Cool in pan on a wire rack 15 minutes; remove cake from pan, and cool completely on wire rack. Spoon glaze over top of cake.

Yield: 1 (10-inch) cake.

Chocolate Glaze

3   (1-ounce) unsweetened chocolate baking squares, melted
1½   cups sifted powdered sugar
¼   cup hot water
½   cup egg substitute
¼   cup butter or margarine, softened

Combine melted chocolate, sugar, and water; beat at medium speed with an electric mixer until blended. Gradually add egg substitute, and beat until mixture cools. Add butter, 1 tablespoon at a time, beating until blended.

Yield: 1¼ cups.

KITCHEN TIPS

Measuring Ingredients

Liquid measuring cups have a rim above the measuring line to keep liquid ingredients from spilling. Nested measuring cups are used to measure dry ingredients, shortening, and peanut butter. Measuring spoons are used for measuring both dry and liquid ingredients.

To measure flour or granulated sugar: Spoon ingredient into nested measuring cup, and level off with a knife. Do not pack down with spoon.

To measure powdered sugar: Lightly spoon sugar into nested measuring cup, and level off with a knife.

To measure brown sugar: Pack sugar into nested measuring cup, and level off with a knife. Sugar should hold its shape when removed from cup.

To measure dry ingredients equaling less than ¼ cup: Dip measuring spoon into ingredient, and level off with a knife.

To measure shortening or peanut butter: Pack ingredient firmly into nested measuring cup, and level off with a knife.

To measure liquids: Use a liquid measuring cup placed on a flat surface. Pour ingredient into cup, and check measuring line at eye level.

To measure honey or syrup: For an accurate measurement, lightly spray measuring cup or spoon with vegetable cooking spray before measuring so that liquid will release easily from cup or spoon.

Tests for Candy Making

To determine the correct temperature of cooked candy, use a candy thermometer and the cold water test. Before each use, check the accuracy of your candy thermometer by attaching it to the side of a small saucepan of water, making sure thermometer does not touch bottom of pan. Bring water to a boil. Thermometer should register 212 degrees in boiling water. If it does not, adjust the temperature range for each candy consistency accordingly.

When using a candy thermometer, insert thermometer into candy mixture, making sure thermometer does not touch bottom of pan. Read temperature at eye level. Cook candy to desired temperature range. Working quickly, drop about ½ teaspoon of candy mixture into a cup of ice water. Use a fresh cup of water for each test. Use the following descriptions to determine if candy has reached the correct stage:

Soft Ball Stage (234 to 240 degrees): Candy can be rolled into a soft ball in ice water but will flatten when removed from water.

Firm Ball Stage (242 to 248 degrees): Candy can be rolled into a firm ball in ice water but will flatten if pressed when removed from water.

Hard Ball Stage (250 to 268 degrees): Candy can be rolled into a hard ball in ice water and will remain hard when removed from water.

Soft Crack Stage (270 to 290 degrees): Candy will form hard threads in ice water but will soften when removed from water.

Hard Crack Stage (300 to 310 degrees): Candy will form brittle threads in ice water and will remain brittle when removed from water.

Softening Butter or Margarine

To soften 1 stick, remove wrapper, and place butter on a microwave-safe plate. Microwave on medium-low power (30%) 20 to 30 seconds.

Softening Cream Cheese

To soften cream cheese, remove wrapper, and place cream cheese on a microwave-safe plate. Microwave on medium power (50%) 1 to 1½ minutes for an 8-ounce package or 30 to 45 seconds for a 3-ounce package.

Shredding Cheese

To shred cheese easily, place wrapped cheese in freezer 10 to 20 minutes before shredding.

Toasting Nuts

To toast nuts, spread nuts on an ungreased baking sheet. Stirring occasionally, bake in a 350-degree oven 5 to 8 minutes or until nuts are slightly darker in color.

Preparing Citrus Fruit Zest

To remove the zest (colored outer portion of peel) from citrus fruits, use a fine grater or citrus zester, being careful not to grate bitter white portion of peel.

Toasting Coconut

To toast coconut, spread a thin layer of coconut on an ungreased baking sheet. Stirring occasionally, bake in a 350-degree oven 5 to 7 minutes or until lightly browned.

Melting Candy Coating

To melt candy coating, place chopped coating in top of a double boiler over hot, not boiling, water or in a heavy saucepan over low heat. Stir occasionally with a dry spoon until coating melts. Remove from heat, and use for dipping as desired. To flavor candy coating, add a small amount of flavored oil. To thin, add a small amount of vegetable oil, but no water. If necessary, coating may be returned to heat to remelt.

Melting Chocolate

To melt chocolate, place chopped chocolate in top of a double boiler over hot, not boiling, water or in a heavy saucepan over low heat. Stir occasionally with a dry spoon until chocolate melts. Remove from heat, and use as desired. If necessary, chocolate may be returned to heat to remelt.

Whipping Cream

For greatest volume, chill a glass bowl and beaters before beating whipping cream. In warm weather, place chilled bowl over ice while beating cream.

Substituting Herbs

To substitute fresh herbs for dried, use 1 tablespoon fresh chopped herbs for 1 teaspoon dried herbs.

Cutting Out Cookies

Place a piece of white paper or stencil plastic over pattern. Use a permanent felt-tip pen with a fine point to trace pattern; cut out pattern. Place pattern on rolled-out dough, and use a small sharp knife to cut out cookies. (*Note:* If dough is sticky, frequently dip knife into flour while cutting out cookies.)

EQUIVALENT MEASUREMENTS

1	tablespoon	=	3	teaspoons
⅛	cup (1 fluid ounce)	=	2	tablespoons
¼	cup (2 fluid ounces)	=	4	tablespoons
⅓	cup	=	5⅓	tablespoons
½	cup (4 fluid ounces)	=	8	tablespoons
¾	cup (6 fluid ounces)	=	12	tablespoons
1	cup (8 fluid ounces)	=	16	tablespoons or ½ pint
2	cups (16 fluid ounces)	=	1	pint
1	quart (32 fluid ounces)	=	2	pints
½	gallon (64 fluid ounces)	=	2	quarts
1	gallon (128 fluid ounces)	=	4	quarts

HELPFUL FOOD EQUIVALENTS

½	cup butter	=	1	stick butter
1	square baking chocolate	=	1	ounce chocolate
1	cup chocolate chips	=	6	ounces chocolate chips
2¼	cups packed brown sugar	=	1	pound brown sugar
3½	cups unsifted powdered sugar	=	1	pound powdered sugar
2	cups granulated sugar	=	1	pound granulated sugar
4	cups all-purpose flour	=	1	pound all-purpose flour
1	cup shredded cheese	=	4	ounces cheese
3	cups sliced carrots	=	1	pound carrots
½	cup chopped celery	=	1	celery rib
½	cup chopped onion	=	1	small onion
1	cup chopped green pepper	=	1	large green pepper

RECIPE INDEX
A-C

CREDITS

To the talented people who helped

in the creation of the projects in this book,

we extend a special word of thanks:

Lauren Brooks

Adrienne Davis

Connie Formby

Catherine Fowler

Catherine Pewitt